Let the TRADE WINS FLOW

2nd edition

Dr Harry Stanton

with Louise Bedford and Chris Tate

Published by
The Trading Game Pty Ltd
PO Box 1171
North Caulfield
Victoria 3161
http://tradinggame.com.au

National Library of Australia Cataloguing-in-Publication entry:

Author:	Stanton, Harry G. (Harry Gerald) author.
Title:	Let the trade wins flow / Harry Stanton; Chris Tate; Louise Bedford.
ISBN:	9780992291730 (paperback)
Notes:	Includes bibliographical references and index.
Subjects:	Stocks – Australia.
	Stock exchanges – Australia.
	Investments – Australia.
	Other Authors/Contributors:
	Tate, Chris.
	Bedford, Louise
Dewey Number:	332.632280994

Printed in Australia by Lightning Source
Cover design by Peter Reardon
Interior design by Michael Hanrahan

Disclaimer

CONTENTS

ABOUT THE AUTHORS

Dr Harry Stanton is the author of well over 250 articles and nine books. He was the first ever author to publish an Australian book on positive thinking in 1979. As well as being a practising clinical psychologist, he is recognised as Australia's leading peak-performance coach. In his private practice, he helps clients to manage their lives more successfully by overcoming the obstacles they create within their own minds. In conjunction with Chris Tate and Louise Bedford he has recorded a double CD called *Psychology Secrets* which describes the 10 most common mistakes made by traders and how they might be overcome. Also with Louise Bedford, he has a CD entitled *Relaxation for Traders* which showcases his life-long fascination with hypnosis techniques to help traders overcome anxiety, improve their performance and develop a winning mindset.

Louise Bedford has a serious "hero-worship thing" happening in relation to Dr Harry Stanton. As well as being one of Australia's most compelling speakers on trading, her books – *Trading Secrets, Charting Secrets, The Secret of Candlestick Charting* and *The Secret of Writing Options* – have been on the bestseller lists since 1997. With a degree in psychology, as well as business, she's in an ideal position to run The Mentor Program, in conjunction with her business partner, Chris Tate. The Mentor Program is the most hard-hitting trading education available, that you can repeat for free, crammed into an initial six thought-provoking months. It will provide you with the ability to turn your trading around, and give you everything you need to be a superb trader, across every time-frame, and with every instrument. If you haven't checked it out yet, run over to your computer and tap in www.tradinggame.com.au to see what you've been missing out on.

Chris Tate is considered to be some sort of freaky trading genius by all of his trading peers. He's a trading veteran of over 30 years, one of the first people ever to release a share trading book in Australia and the bestselling author of *The Art of Trading* and *The Art of Options Trading in Australia*. Caustically funny, brutally honest, and capable of making your jaw drop when you hear him present, he is one of the few people who truly understand what does and doesn't work in the markets. He runs a free, irreverent, biting, rebellious daily rant that you simply must sign up for on the Trading Game website (www.tradinggame.com.au).

Together, these three market specialists are a formidable team. Their techniques have helped thousands of traders attain exceptional trading results.

PREFACE

by Louise Bedford

Louise Bedford and Harry Stanton
Your Trading Mentors

My three sisters and my Mum were in turmoil. My father was dying and there was nothing any of us could do about it.

His body was starting to rapidly fade, just the way his mind had over the past few years. Mum's distress was spreading over her like some form of fast-growing cancer. I could feel that we were all very close to dropping into an abyss of despair.

Dad had always been a man who was quick to anger, and explosive in his domineering outbursts. Yet, no matter what sort of confusion this had caused my sisters and I for our entire lives, seeing his spirit deplete and his body crumble was a heck of a lot to bear. Losing a parent is a particular brand of hell.

I rang Harry. My friend. My confidante. My mentor.

He was one of the few people in this world who knows my heart. He also fully grasped the mixed bundle of feelings that my father's presence brought to my life.

Harry arranged to fly in from Tasmania to my home in Melbourne, so we could be together.

By the time he arrived, my father had passed away and I needed Harry more than ever.

You see ... Harry has always been in the background of my life. Influencing my decisions. Encouraging me – even before we met.

When I was an unruly, surly 15 years old, ready to fly off the rails and run away from home, at the urging of my sister Valerie, I read one of Harry's books. His words soothed me and made me feel less alone. His book spoke to my heart.

Suddenly, I knew what I needed to do with my life. After the first three pages of his book, I decided I'd found my calling. I became determined to study psychology at university, so I could gain an insight into how people's minds worked. And how my mind worked.

Little did I know that many years later, Harry would become my friend.

In 1997, my broker introduced us. I was overjoyed to meet Harry, and we clicked immediately. Harry shared his views about options and candles with me, and our friendship deepened. Those topics are two of my hot buttons, that's for sure. He bubbled forth his wisdom gathered over a lifetime of being an internationally famous author, a hypnotist, and Australia's most recognised psychologist to traders. His insights flowed over me like a warm bath of unconditional support.

My desperate yearning for a kind, caring, father-like figure was satisfied.

As a result, the pressure I'd applied to my own father dissipated. As adults, our father/daughter relationship improved greatly. I was still wary though. I made sure that I sheltered my children from the abuse I'd received as a child. This was essential.

My children saw the best of their Grandfather, without having to endure fear, or the pain of an estrangement from one of their relatives.

Harry helped me break the chain.

I believe that if you aren't born into the family you deserve, it just means you drew the short straw in life's lottery. It's then up to you to choose your own family. You can rebuild the support and care that you should have received, if this was denied to you as a child.

Who have you chosen to be your 'family'?

Have you made a conscious choice about who you want to associate with, or do people slip into and out of your life by default? Out of those two strategies, I guarantee that only one will help your long-term future.

LET THE TRADE WINS FLOW

I chose Harry to be a part of my family. I am indebted to him for the healing he has brought to my life. His belief and care for me take my breath away.

I am honoured to bring you this new edition of Dr Harry Stanton's book *Let the Trade Wins Flow*. You need to read carefully every word this man has written. His ability to create life changes in those who follow his work is nothing short of remarkable.

May his words seep into your thoughts and your heart, so that you reap the rewards the market stockpiles for traders who have the discipline to follow their trading plans.

Re-publishing Harry's book has been a labour of love.

I'm going to hand you over to Harry now so you can experience why I attribute him with changing the very direction of my life.

Louise Bedford
January 2014

CHAPTER 1

HOW PSYCHOLOGY CAN HELP THE TRADER

'The tragedy in life doesn't lie in not reaching your goal.
The tragedy lies in having no goal to reach.'

– Benjamin Mays

INTRODUCTION

It's Harry Stanton here. I want to prepare you for what you're going to discover over the next 13 chapters.

This is a very practical book. It focuses on how we can use our minds to help us become successful traders.

I'll discuss things that work. These techniques can be employed to produce positive results, even if there may not be a theory available to explain why they work.

This book does more than show you how psychology can help you trade more successfully. It is about winning in life generally.

The skills and techniques described in these pages will help you manage your life more successfully, gaining increased control over your thoughts, your feelings and your behaviour. This, in turn, will make you a better trader.

Trading is one part of your life, and it is the one emphasised in this book, with most of the examples used being drawn from this field. However, you will miss much of its value if you restrict your focus to trading alone. Not generalising the knowledge you gain to all other aspects of your life is a mistake. Similarly, you will almost certainly fail to achieve your full trading potential if you have a life that lacks balance and purpose.

1

Psychology alone, however, will not make you a great trader. You need to invest in your own education.

▷ You require clear-cut entry, exit and trade-management rules, such as those created by Louise Bedford and Chris Tate in their Mentor Program. This will help remove the uncertainty and the indecisiveness, which is a prime cause of failure both in trading and in virtually all other aspects of our lives.

When you link precise money-management rules to the use of such a system, you move yourself further along the path to success. By doing this, you position yourself to derive immense personal power from the psychological approaches I describe. This power can make you a superb trader.

▷ Just a quick definition – a 'trading system' defines your entry, exit and position-sizing rules. Every effective trader has a written trading system, and it's their goal to follow that system without question.

WHY IS PSYCHOLOGY IMPORTANT?

Let's look at why psychology does play such an important part in the art of trading.

▷ Professional traders are virtually unanimous in maintaining that the most difficult part of trading is the psychological aspects. You see, emotions can so easily interfere with trading.

One of the most common ways in which this occurs is that traders, despite having a clear-cut system, are influenced by external factors. They make the assumption that some 'expert' knows more than they do about the imminent direction of prices. They then proceed to override their rules. If you are to achieve success as a trader, you must learn to ▷ trust yourself and your proven system, ignoring these highly fallible outside influences and following your rules exactly.

I recall the story told by Curtis Arnold about the well-known system developer who, at a trading seminar, taught a winning system to a large number of participants. These people paid thousands of dollars to learn it. This trading approach was monitored by a third party.

One year later, it was shown to have performed extremely well. Yet, a survey of those attendees showed that less than 10 per cent of them ▷ were using the system at this time. So here we have a group of people who paid a lot of money to learn a system that had proven to be very successful, yet they were no longer using it. As Arnold says, 'the reason has little to do with the system but has a lot to do with discipline'.

This story demonstrates unequivocally that possession of a really good trading system is not enough. It is the discipline to follow the system's rules consistently that is of equal importance for there are many ways in which we can defeat a system.

These include taking some trades and ignoring others because we just know the index is going higher, trading too many contracts because we know the market is due to take off, and being lazy in that we'll put our stop-loss order in tomorrow. We may even hope for divine intervention as we change our stop to allow more room for our trade to work, because of something we may have read in the papers. We often fear for the worst when the system says to stay with our position.

In fact, emotional discipline may be even more important than having a good system. Writing in his very popular book *The New Market Wizards*, Jack Schwager put it this way:

> If there is a single theme that keeps recurring in this volume, as it did in *Market Wizards*, it is that psychology is critical to success at trading. In order to achieve success in life, you must have the right mental attitude.
>
> If trading (or any other endeavour) is a source of anxiety, fear, frustration, depression, or anger, something is wrong – even if you are successful in the conventional sense, and especially if you're not. You have to enjoy trading, because if trading is a source of negative emotions, you have probably already lost the game, even if you make money.

Many people keep doing things they do not enjoy; things that make them anxious and frightened. Sometimes they may have no control over this situation, but much more frequently they inflict this situation upon themselves.

Schwager believes that a very accurate summary of trading is encapsulated in the famous quote from Walt Kelly's cartoon strip *Pogo*: 'We have met the enemy and it is us'.

We are, it would appear, our own worst enemies, and to improve our lives and our trading we have to look within, rather than to blame outside forces for our failures.

The outstandingly successful traders who were interviewed for *The New Market Wizards* and its predecessor, *Market Wizards,* stressed the absolutely critical role of psychological elements. What does become abundantly obvious when reading these two books and the ideas of the traders who had reached the pinnacle of their profession is that, when asked to explain what was important to success, these Market Wizards never talked about indicators or techniques. Rather, they talked about such things as discipline, emotional control, patience, and mental attitude toward losing. Again the message is clear: the key to winning in the markets is internal, not external.

'WHAT IS' AND WHAT YOU ADD TO 'WHAT IS'

Jerry, a 28-year-old businessman who had been trading on a part-time basis for two years, is fairly typical of many traders. Most of his time and his efforts were directed into the search for the really great trades. When he thought he had found such a trade, he made his entry. Then he experienced constant emotional swings between exultation as the trade went well and black despair as it turned sour. Locked into this emotional turmoil, Jerry was totally unable to use the experience as a means of learning how to take more control over his life.

The emotional swings of traders

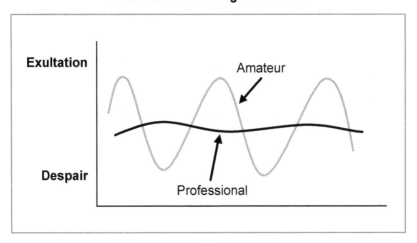

Philosophers, since the birth of time, have taught that every event occurring in our lives provides the opportunity for growth and for learning about ourselves. Our inherent goal is to become what we are truly capable of being.

Winning professionals have already learnt this lesson, accepting the total necessity of concentrating on 'what is', instead of siphoning off energy into emotional excesses of joy and despair. They accept the reality of the market rather than bemoaning what might have been or what could possibly be.

Yet even winning professionals have their problems psychologically. Though they may trade very profitably for the institutions that employ them, should they leave in order to trade for themselves, very few actually achieve any great success. Like us, they find that the emotions of fear, greed, and hope still prevail, generating exhilaration and misery when their own money is at stake. This is a very clear indication that psychology is the key to trading success or failure. If it were not, these traders would do equally well with their own money as they had with that of the institution.

Hope and fear are two of the greatest enemies of the speculator, fostering only false perceptions. Hoping that a trade will go your way, or fearing that it will not, are attitudes that lead to unrealistic expectations, emotional decisions, and negative attitudes. Once the trade has been made, its fate is sealed and no amount of hope, or fear, will make things any different.

Alexander Elder in *Trading for a Living* subscribes to the view that emotional factors are of vital importance in determining whether a trader will succeed or fail. Interestingly, he also draws attention to the way in which markets are actually set up so that most traders must lose money.

He highlights the fact, often overlooked by traders, that trading is a minus-sum game in which, because commissions and slippage drain huge amounts of money from the market, winners receive less than the amounts lost by the losers. Therefore it is not enough to be a good, 'average trader'. To win a minus-sum game, it is necessary to be vastly superior to the crowd, and to achieve this superiority it is essential to be in control of your emotions.

This concept of the minus-sum game may be true of futures trading, but it is not really valid in the sharemarket. In equities, no-one need ever lose if prices keep rising and the person investing is prepared to hold on for a sufficiently long period of time. However, despite this caveat about Elder's position, he has posed the real challenge of the markets and it is one that the techniques outlined in this book should help you meet.

TATE ON TRADING

To add to the information Harry is providing you about the markets, from time to time Louise Bedford and I intend to add our two bobs about the markets. That way you'll get the benefit from all three of us.

You may already know a little bit about me, as well as Louise Bedford. Together, we've been running our Mentor Program since the year 2000. I've been trading since the 80s, and Louise has been trading since the early 90s. We aim to drive your trading to the next level, and provoke and prod you towards trading success.

Enough throat clearing…let me add to Harry's thoughts…

Typically when a trader enters the market for the first time they start thinking about how much money they will make. The reality is that a new trader may never make any money because 'reward' is a phantom that may never exist.

▷ The only constant in markets is risk.

Despite the current vogue in stock market advertising there is no such thing as a risk-less trade. Markets only operate because of the risk/
▷ reward equation. No risk, no reward.

▷ Risk can never be eliminated, only managed. Professionals have always known this and it is reflected in the approach they take, which is not to make money but to minimise the amount they can possibly lose.

It is imperative that as a trader you have a rules-based approach to the market for two reasons. Firstly, there are no rules for trading imposed upon you. The market has no rules for how you should trade. Any
▷ rules you generate are your own; as such they have to suit your objectives as a trader and your personal approach to the market.

▷ Secondly, having rules removes the evils of emotion from trading.

Many traders have the wrong idea about trading. They assume that it is some testosterone-driven environment where there is a lot of yelling and screaming each day and that it is a confrontation that needs to be won. Nothing could be further from the truth. Trading is a calm, disciplined profession. The moment your emotions creep into trading you are lost.

Certainly the popular image of trading is one of a very boisterous environment, generally dominated by males. However, this image is a false one.

Unfortunately it infects the psyche of a trader and leads them towards failure. It also acts as a barrier to women who want to enter trading as a career. (Such a development is unfortunate because the available
▷ evidence suggests that women are better traders than men.)

Make no mistake: traders must have a trading system. If you have no system you will fail. However, unless you get your own psychology right in the markets, you will end up doing the wrong thing, time and time again.

Keep reading to hear why some people should avoid the market like the plague ...

CHAPTER 2

THE CHALLENGE OF THE MARKETS

'Success consists of going from failure to
failure without loss of enthusiasm.'

– Winston Churchill

SELF-REALISATION AND THE MARKET

It is the challenge of the markets that motivates us to trade. It provides the powerful drive to achieve the best of which we are capable, relative to our inner potentials.

The market provides us with an arena in which to test ourselves, and to tap into strengths within ourselves we have not been using. In *The Disciplined Trader,* Mark Douglas puts it this way: 'The traders who can make money consistently approach trading from the perspective of a mental discipline'.

As Elder has so astutely pointed out, it is this need for self-realisation that is probably more important than the pleasure of the trading game itself and the reward of money. The goal of good traders, he believes, is to trade well. If they do so, money follows almost as an afterthought.

Successful traders are continually striving to be the best traders they can be. This is of more importance than making money. The power of greed and fear is vastly reduced if you approach the markets with this attitude.

Unfortunately, this is not the way it is for most people. Trading so often provides a magnetic lure for the type of person who should avoid the market like the plague.

These are the ones who act on impulse – the gamblers, the plungers who trade for the excitement and the adrenalin rush. Yet when these traders lose money, as they invariably do, they rarely take personal responsibility for their failure. Rather, they direct their blame towards others, attributing their losses to bad luck or poor advice rather than to their own arrogance, egoism, fear, and greed.

It is not luck or the quality of the advice you receive that determines your success or failure as a trader. It is your ability to control your emotions. Every trade you make is your responsibility, not someone else's. You and only you decide when to enter and when to exit.

Taking such responsibility can be difficult, faced with the temptations of the market. They offer the promise of vast profits, invoking our greed while, at the same time, also invoking a very high level of fear. On the one hand we want huge profits; on the other we fear losing the money we already have.

Success or failure in the market is often dependent upon your attitudes towards the emotions of fear and greed. Your views about the prospect of gain and the risk of loss and towards the excitement of trading itself will determine how you perceive the markets.

Should you be carried away with the adrenalin rush rather than adopting a more detached, unemotional attitude, you are likely to experience trouble.

As Elder has commented, the trader who feels overjoyed when he wins, and depressed when he loses, cannot accumulate equity because he is controlled by his emotions.

> If you let the market make you feel high or low, you will lose money... The market is like an ocean – it moves up and down regardless of what you want. You may feel joy when you buy a stock and it explodes in a rally. You may feel drenched with fear when you go short but the market rises and your equity melts with every uptick.

> These feelings have nothing to do with the market – they exist only inside you. The market does not know you exist. You can do nothing to influence it.

> You can only control your behaviour. Your feelings about the ocean exist only in your mind. They threaten your survival when you let your feelings rather than your intellect control your behaviour.

> You can never control the market but you can learn to control yourself.

a woman

A TRIED AND TRUE METHOD

One way to achieve this goal is through the use of self-reward. Every time you actually do the correct thing, such as entering a trade in accordance with your system or exiting at the appropriate point, reward yourself immediately.

If, on the other hand, you realise that you have broken your rules – that is, you have done the incorrect thing – immediately go back in your mind and mentally replay the event, this time doing it the way you know it should have been handled.

Your attitude is all-important and can well be your greatest asset. Because the emotional enemies of profitable trading are constantly with you, it is essential that you maintain a positive attitude. You need to develop an attitude that supports you with positive, cheerful, and optimistic thoughts, irrespective of the negative effects of losses, interference from other people, and poor trading signals. You must believe that you are a winner. In your gut, you must feel you are someone who will succeed, despite these negative factors.

Support counts

To maintain such an attitude you need to surround yourself with winners. Positive attitudes are catching, and if we associate with people who are highly motivated, ambitious, goal-oriented, and who see obstacles as challenges to be overcome, we are likely to take on this view ourselves.

As has often been said, if you want to fly with the eagles, don't hang out with the turkeys. Avoid the losers, the complainers, and the negative thinkers like the plague. They can infect you with their own losing mentality.

Some traders read charts well, applying technical analysis that allows them to tell you exactly what the market will do next. Sometimes they are correct. However, although they may have a very good system for trading, they do not prosper because when it actually comes to putting on the trade with their own money, their intellectual coolness departs.

The pressure engendered by taking action which may result in the loss of money becomes so great that their judgement is overridden by their emotions. They have become unable to 'pull the trigger', and do not place the trades they have identified as likely to be profitable.

Over-confidence is also a killer

Becoming overconfident is the other side of the coin – one which can lead you into the self-destructive behaviour of overtrading.

The market has its rhythm. There are times when it runs for you as if you cannot go wrong – and there are also times when, no matter what you do, it all goes wrong.

Just as you strengthen yourself so that the bad times are not permitted to destroy you, so too you must not permit the good times to over-excite you.

Trading while in a state of great excitement can be disastrous. Winning can create such exhilaration that you get carried away, swept up in the excitement of trading, losing control.

Through practising detachment – the self-awareness that is the main theme of this book – you will come to even out the peaks and troughs, to trade calmly, less emotionally.

THE POWER OF DETACHMENT

Detachment is easier to practise if you adopt a style of trading that fits your own personality. This usually means one that causes the least anxiety.

Since stress, tension, and anxiety tend to lead into losing trades, anything you can do to lessen these states is advisable.

The best trading system is the one that allows you to sleep easily at night. If you lie awake worrying about your trades, you are using a method out of harmony with your personality. This is likely to increase both your stress level and your losses.

On many occasions it is overtrading, or taking on too much risk, that is causing the sleep disturbance.

It has often been said that the three most important factors in the real estate business are location, location, and location. Perhaps this could be paraphrased as: the three most important factors in trading are undertrade, undertrade, and undertrade.

If you never trade so heavily that you jeopardise your lifestyle, you will not only sleep far better but are far more likely to remain in the game. Knowing your worst possible outcome achieves the same purpose.

It is something of a truism in the world of trading that even though you can only make an estimate of your likely reward on a particular trade, you can quantify your risk far more precisely. If, before taking a position, you always know the amount you are willing to lose, you remove much of the tension from your trading.

You should also tap into one of the great secrets of being successful in the market. When you are wrong, minimise your losses so that you can play another day. Stop-loss orders and learning the rules of money management allow you to do this automatically.

Getting hit by large losses undermines confidence and creates emotional turmoil. This latter state often predisposes traders to try to get back their losses immediately, usually through overtrading. This is virtually a sure way to fail. The opposite tack is likely to be a lot more productive. That is, after a big loss, play small, looking for any sort of profit at all.

get back on the horse

FEAR AND GREED

Fear and greed make it difficult for traders to behave in a rational way.

Fear pushes us to either hold on to losing positions too long or to get out of winning positions too early that later become highly profitable. Conversely, greed for those few extra ticks pushes us into holding on to positions we should be exiting.

One approach to sublimating fear and greed is that of desensitisation. The more you trade over time, the less of a grip fear and greed will have over you. The key here is to only trade small amounts.

Because the amounts you bet may be small, you can reach a stage when you do not really care if you win or lose.

With continual repetition of this process, you can achieve insensitivity about what happens to money. That is, your emotions have become dulled in this area and you do not react emotionally to the results you are getting. Paper trading where you don't have real money in the markets may help you get part of the way there – but there's nothing like having real money on the line.

BECOME MORE 'ZEN'

Another approach is to accept the reality that nothing really matters. Zen philosophy embodies the concept of letting it happen, or not attempting to push the river.

Marcus Aurelius, the Roman emperor, adopted the fatalistic view that whatever is due to happen will happen. Such a philosophy affirms that the only real problem in life lies in our mind.

Nothing has value except the value we attach to it. The phrase 'it's only money' expresses this view. It is possible to achieve a state in which there's a sense of nothingness to money, or market success or failures. Whatever the market chooses to do or not do has no value. Because it has no value, there is nothing to fear.

You cannot be fearful of losing nothing, nor can you be greedy about gaining something that is nothing. When we attach importance to something, we give it power over us. With the money and the market, attaching importance to them creates the very fear and greed which can be our undoing.

It is not easy to achieve this detachment. This acceptance that the market is not worthy of your emotional involvement is difficult. Once you have taken a position, you have made a mental and ego commitment to the market, one that is very difficult to abandon. We hang on to hard-gained views.

Let's say, after careful study, you have made a judgement about what the market is going to do. When you commit yourself to this view, you seek further reasons why the position will prove profitable. You enter the market in accordance with your view. Should the trade turn against you, instead of recognising that the market is telling you that you are wrong, your mind keeps coming up with all the more reasons why you should stay with the position.

Ignore these. Listen to the market.

It tells you very clearly that you were wrong in your judgement. It tells you to either liquidate your position or reverse it so that you get back in harmony with the market.

If you're losing money, then the market is doing the opposite to what you predicted, so you should be out of the trade.

BUT IT'S HARD BEING WRONG ...

It is hard for us to accept that we are wrong. Our ego is involved. After all, we have done all this meticulous technical analysis and we know the market is going to move up. Unfortunately this 'knowing' prevents us observing the information that tells us that if we stick to our judgement, we are going to lose a lot of money.

It is really a matter of whether making money is more important to you than being right. Though this may seem an easy choice to make, in practice it often is quite difficult, for being right, not making mistakes, can be essential to a person's self-image.

Admitting to error is, for such a person, extremely damaging to a trader's self-esteem, and losing money may be more acceptable than facing the error of judgement.

In a losing position, such traders might think: 'I'll get out when I'm even'. Why should getting even be so important? Perhaps because it would save a loss but probably, more importantly, because it would protect the ego.

Fragile egos that need the constant support of being right will find the marketplace provides a very rough ride! However, should you adopt the view expressed earlier, that the market is an excellent opportunity for self-development, then you may come to realise that making money is a lot more enjoyable than being right.

As I indicated earlier, when you have followed your system exactly, regardless of whether the trade was a winner or a loser, reward yourself. Never reward yourself after a winning trade if you failed to follow your system's rules.

After completion of a trade, study what you did very carefully. Review your written reasons for making the trade, and, also in writing, in what way you failed to implement your plan for the trade, and why. Also note your feeling about it at the time of entry and during its progress, particularly if, at some time, it moved against you.

In this way you will become very aware of the common factors, those that are always present whenever you make a winning trade. Although many books advise you to do this type of meticulous study primarily on your losers, it is better for your confidence to focus more attention on your winners than your losers – though you do need to analyse both. By doing so, you maintain a winning rather than a losing focus.

LOUISE'S THOUGHTS

When I first read this book, some of Harry's ideas seemed a bit whacky to me – even though I was already one of his biggest fans. I remember reading his thoughts about 'the pendulum', which you'll read about in just a few pages. I actually said to myself: 'You've got to be kidding!'

However, over the years I found myself referring to this book continually. Slowly my mind began to open up. Just a little at first, and then I began to embrace his methods so fully, they became a part of my unconscious.

Finally, I was prepared to take Harry's words and implement them.

I pretended Harry was my personal trading coach. Everything he suggested, I did without question. Every method he suggested, I suspended skepticism, and I implemented.

If we all had a personal trading coach, I'm sure that we would detect our own flaws and strengths, and improve our strategies, with overwhelming speed. Depending on how you use this book, you could be at the brink of achieving feats you can currently hardly believe are possible. Sometimes it takes someone just a few paces further ahead of you to help you realise what is possible.

Because trading is largely a solitary occupation, you will need to be responsible for your own trading development. Achieving objectivity is a difficult prospect. You will accomplish trading excellence by regularly analysing your own strengths and weaknesses.

As soon as I finished reading *Let the Trade Wins Flow* for the first time, I created a trading diary so that I could record everything about each trade I made.

I bought an A4 ring-binder folder, and assigned one page to each share that I bought.

You'll find that all of the most successful traders use some form of recording their trading history. You should too.

Before entering a trade, I recorded all of my thoughts and analysis. Unless I can justify my trade on paper, I did not enter the position.

I suggest that you imagine you are trying to convince another person, who is incredibly skeptical about shares, to buy a particular share. If you could win such an argument, go ahead and buy the share.

It is essential to keep your records in date order and to separate your completed transactions for each trading month. After each trade has been completed, write down your profit, your loss, the amount of time that you held the share, and the main lessons that you have learned.

After making a profit or a loss, I record my answers to the following questions:

- What did I do well?

- What would I do differently if I repeated this trade?

You may choose to use some form of electronic method of keeping track of your trades. This is also viable.

Whichever method you use, make it your own. It will save you a fortune in the long run.

You see … unfortunately, some traders must go through some sort of catastrophe to finally get their own attention, and make an effort to improve their system. Psychologists call this 'one-trial learning'. The one experience is so excruciatingly devastating that it results in an instant change in behaviour – painful, yet effective.

A quick whack to the side of the head can sometimes be the best thing to ever happen to you, as long as your head doesn't get completely knocked off in the process.

Keep reading and Harry will show you how to gain some perspective …

CHAPTER 3

GAINING A SENSE
OF PROPORTION

'By recording your dreams and goals on paper, you set in
motion the process of becoming the person you most
want to be. Put your future in good hands – your own.'

– Mark Victor Hansen

THE MENTAL PERCEPTION SCALE

Whether we are winning or losing, we need to develop a sense of proportion. A useful exercise to help you achieve this involves the use of
a perception scale, running from 0 to 10, which you see in your mind.

Mental perception scale

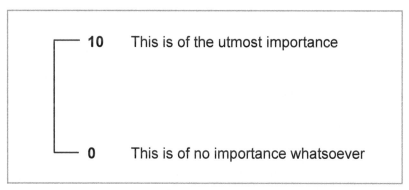

Let's say you make a long-range forecast for the Swiss Franc to top on
January 12th of next year. Everything seems to be coming together very
nicely and you are quite convinced the top will arrive at the scheduled
time on the scheduled date.

On January 12th, when your trading system gives a sell signal, you place your order to go short, get set and then, with a sense of increasing horror, see the price climb steeply.

You are angry that the currency didn't do as you expected it to do. The psychological problem of the ego rears its ugly head, and you are very upset at the big loss you take. Even though your stop closed the trade quickly, the rise was so rapid that the price at which you did get out was far worse than the one you had anticipated.

It is easy to make an event such as this a 10 on the Mental Perception Scale. You build it up to be a tremendous tragedy; a real catastrophe. To put it into a more realistic context, ask yourself questions such as:

▸ 'If I became totally paralysed in a car accident, where would that rate on the scale?'

▸ 'If my son or daughter died from a drug overdose, where would that rate?'

▸ 'If I lived in a country where each day could be my last because of the butchery of civil war, where would I put that on the scale?'

Doing such an exercise gives you breathing time, helping you to calm down a little after your unpleasant incursion into the currency market. It contributes to placing the event itself in perspective. It allows you to become more objective about how important it actually is.

I well remember an occasion when I was conducting a seminar on stress management for a group of business executives at which I had just explained this scale idea. One man, who had previously consulted me on an individual basis, told the group that his wife had died four years ago leaving him with two young children to bring up. He felt this was the worst thing that could have happened to him. This was a 10.

Since then, he had never rated anything, no matter how stressful others may have found it, higher than a 2. All the pressures upsetting his colleagues had little effect on him because, by comparison with his wife's death, they just didn't really matter. Accordingly, he handled them much better than his more highly stressed colleagues.

This man had turned something very negative into something very positive, transforming the pain of loss into the ability to handle stress very successfully. This ability to transform negatives into positives is one of the real secrets of achieving mastery over your life.

Applying the scale in other ways

The use of the Mental Perception Scale can be expanded to areas such as the control of anxiety and pain. Let's say you feel very tense. If you wish to feel more comfortable, more at ease, sit down quietly and look up into the corner of your mind, and notice the number that is associated with the level of tension you feel.

The higher the number, the greater the tension.

Then, just watch as the number begins to change. How this will happen is likely to vary for different individuals, but probably the most common way for it to occur is that the number slowly fades from your visual awareness, and as it does so a smaller number will emerge from the background.

Let me be more specific.

If you feel and see an '8', you may begin to notice the lines of the '8' begin to fade, and '7' will become more apparent. Or maybe the curves of the '8' will begin to straighten, and become more like the angles of the '7', until, after a while, the angularity of the '7' will take on the graceful curves of the '6'.

It could be that the '6' will, like the pages of a calendar in a movie, be blown off by the wind into the darkness, leaving a '5'.

Perhaps the '5' will begin to open, ever so gradually, and the line at the top will fade until you notice there is no longer really a '5' there but rather a '4'.

Some numbers might be skipped altogether, and you might, more quickly than you expect, begin to have the impression of a lovely white swan, gliding along, the graceful long curve of its neck reminding you very, very distinctly of a '2'.

Or is it that, seeing a '2', you are reminded of a swan. And not only reminded of a swan, but, somehow, begin to feel almost as if you, too, are gliding gently along, the smoothness and grace more and more a part of your awareness.

You may even find the curve of the swan's neck straightening out to become a '1' and the straight line of the '1' bulging out to become a '0', at which point you achieve an oceanic feeling, a sense of oneness and harmony with the universe.

If you were using this idea to reduce pain, it would be wise to reduce it only to about the '2' level as pain is a signal, a constant reminder, that something is wrong that requires attention.

Become more comfortable – straight away

So any time that you wish to feel more comfortable, look up into the corner of your mind and see the number you feel. Then just watch, as the numbers, and your feelings, begin to change.

This method may also be used to improve your performance over a whole range of activities. Let us imagine you enter a trade according to your entry and exit rules.

You are sharp, thinking clearly and acting decisively. In other words, you are at the top of your form.

At such times, when you feel at your best, look up in the corner of your mind and see the number that is there. You will find it is always the same number and this is your optimal performance level. Perhaps it is a 7.

In future, when you need to be at your best, as when you are sitting down to analyse your charts, look up into your mind and see the number that is there. If it is a 7, you can feel confident you are in the frame of mind to generate your best performance.

Should the number be lower, say a 4, change the number in the way I have described above. You may care to link the number changing to your breathing. As you change each number upwards, make this change as you breathe in energy and vitality.

Should the number be too high, say a 9, change the number downward, making each change as you breathe out tension and strain. In this way you can always be at your best when you need to be.

Placing yourself at your optimum number helps you achieve a more powerful motivational state.

THE VALUE OF YOUR UNCONSCIOUS MIND

The work you do and the decisions you make are not only the arena of your conscious mind. Pay attention to intuition also. This is a controversial topic, so I must warn you that it only has bearing if you're already a successful trader. Too many traders confuse a beginner's gut feel with the intuition of an expert trader.

Intuition is basically experience that resides in the unconscious mind.

It would appear that everything that happens to us in our lives is recorded by this mind. The unfortunate aspect of this is that every time you have a losing trade, the memory is etched in your unconscious. The more losses you have, the deeper the impression and the deeper the pain.

In fact, substantial losses generated by a previous trading system can make a powerful impression on your unconscious. It may be such a dramatic effect that whenever you contemplate making a trade with a new trading system, the fear of executing the trade becomes so great that you are immobilised. Analysis paralysis strikes at many traders and is something you need to avoid at all costs.

The coin toss

Fortunately, there is a very positive side to the unconscious mind. You can gain access to its wisdom in a number of quite simple ways.

One of these is through tossing a coin.

Take decision-making as an example. Every day we have to make many, many decisions, and often we agonise for hours before deciding what to do. Then we fret that we have not made the correct decision.

But most of these decisions that cause us so much mental anguish are totally trivial. They really don't matter all that much, and if we happen to decide incorrectly it is usually quite easy to rectify the mistake.

Most decisions are between two alternatives, A or B. If you cannot make up your mind, toss a coin.

When the coin is in the air you will know which way you want it to come down. This is your decision.

You don't have to look at which way the coin has fallen because, while it was in the air, your unconscious mind gave you the information you needed to make your decision.

THE PENDULUM

If you can accept my earlier point that almost all of our decisions are both trivial and reversible, then you will find the following technique, which involves using a simple pendulum, an excellent way of making a choice. I know Louise Bedford scoffed at this method when she was first introduced to it. However, persist, and you'll see why it's a method that can simplify your decision-making.

What you're about to do is hand the decision-making process over to the pendulum – so you no longer have to fret about making the 'right' choice.

I have been using the pendulum for over fifty years and have come to accept without question that the pendulum makes better decisions for me than I can make for myself. It mitigates the effects of the so-called rational processes we are taught to use.

The reason is simple: no matter how carefully we weigh up alternatives, we never have access to all the relevant information.

Through use of the pendulum I believe we are tapping into a source which has access to much greater information and this enables better decisions to be made. In theory, this is because we are getting in touch with our unconscious minds.

How this method works

As I mentioned earlier, it has been widely suggested that from the moment we are born every experience we have is recorded in the unconscious mind. Though consciously we have forgotten most of this material, the unconscious mind retains it all. When we request information by means of the pendulum, it is able to draw on this vast reservoir of knowledge to provide an answer.

It is this same process that occurs when we come to a decision through rational problem-solving methods, yet something inside tells us we are wrong. Hunches or intuitions like this are to be ignored at your peril for they usually prove to be correct.

The pendulum can be any small object such as a ring, a key, a small piece of gemstone, a crystal, or a medallion. A thread, perhaps of nylon or cotton, is tied to this object. The length is usually about 20 to 25 centimetres. The thread is held between thumb and forefinger, about 5 to 8 centimetres away from the pendulum bob. The remainder of the thread is wrapped around your fingers out of the way.

With the pendulum suspended from your fingers in this way, bend your elbow so that the forearm is approximately parallel with the ground. You may rest your elbow on a chair arm or table or leave it unsupported. Next swing the pendulum about, to and fro, clockwise and anticlockwise, keeping all movement of fingers, hand and arm to a minimum.

As you do so, vary the length of the thread until you find a position which seems natural for you. Four basic movements of the pendulum are possible. These are:

▶ a back-and-forth movement in front of you, from left to right and right to left, across your body

▶ a to-and-fro movement towards your body and then away

▶ a circular clockwise movement

▶ a circular anti-clockwise movement.

Your inner mind can be asked to make its own selection from among these movements, so that a specific response is attached to each one. One movement is to signify 'yes', a second 'no', a third 'don't know', and a fourth 'I don't want to answer the question'.

Sort out a 'yes' from a 'no'

To sort out for yourself which movement means 'yes', ask the pendulum. Adopting an attitude of neutrality, of detachment, think 'yes' to yourself while watching the pendulum.

Alternatively you might, if your name is John Chalmers, ask: 'Is my name John Chalmers?' Observe the movement of the pendulum in response to this question.

This is your 'yes' answer. Run a couple of similar tests to definitely establish that this response is the correct one. Then think 'no' or ask: 'Is my name Charlie Jones?' to identify your 'no' response.

Test this with other questions.

Now, try thinking 'I don't know' as you watch the pendulum to establish your third movement, and 'I don't want to answer' for the fourth.

Once you establish the meaning of the pendulum movement to your satisfaction, you can then put it to use.

When faced with a decision, review the information you have available and ask the pendulum what would be best for you to do. Perhaps you are unable to make up your mind whether it would be best for you to concentrate entirely upon one contract, such as a stock market index, or whether to spread yourself widely over many markets.

You could pose this question: 'Is it advisable for me to concentrate on one market only rather than to trade many markets?' When you receive an answer via the pendulum swing, check this by reversing your question: 'Is it advisable for me to trade many markets rather than to concentrate on one market only?' Hopefully, the two answers you receive will be consistent, one 'yes' and one 'no'.

If you do not receive a clear answer, the reason usually lies in the way you have framed your question. It may not be sufficiently precise. Sometimes the pendulum will tell you this by swinging diagonally, or by repeatedly indicating the 'I don't know' response.

Should this occur, reframe your question making it more exact, more literal. A correctly phrased question is a problem half solved.

As you become increasingly familiar with the pendulum and its movements, you will develop considerable confidence in its decision-making ability. Accordingly, when you fail to receive the appropriate response, you will tend to look more for some error in your own questioning technique rather than to blame the pendulum itself.

When does this work?

You will probably find that the pendulum works better on some occasions than on others. That is why it is a good idea to let it tell you when it is ready for decision-making.

Ask it, 'If you are willing to help me make a decision about (whatever your concern is), indicate by giving me a "yes" signal. If, at this moment, you are unwilling to make such a decision, indicate with a "no" signal.'

Should you get the 'no' signal, leave the pendulum for the moment and try again, say, half an hour later. You cannot force the process – wait until the pendulum is ready for you, as it will be most of the time. Maintain a detached attitude as you pose your question and await an answer.

Once you have an answer, put it into action and forget it. Do not waste time second-guessing, wondering what would have happened if the pendulum had made some other choice. The whole idea of using the pendulum is to turn off such useless agonising and to spare you the worries of uncertainty which are probably far worse than the consequences of making a poor decision.

Indecision causes us to feel stressed and pressured, and makes our lives less pleasant than they otherwise would be.

The great virtue of the pendulum is that it removes this indecision.

ANOTHER WAY TO USE YOUR UNCONSCIOUS SIGNALS

A third way of communicating with your unconscious mind is to use the following procedure. Place yourself in a relaxed state. Perhaps the easiest way of doing this is to become aware of the rhythm of your own breathing, watching it flow in and out without interruption. It's almost as if you were actually watching someone else breathing. On the out-breath, let go of tension, stress, and pressure. Allow the breath to take away such things, and then use the following three-step procedure:

1. 'If my unconscious mind is willing to consider the problem, it will give me a signal.'

2. 'When my unconscious mind has explored and examined all the reasons for the problem, it will give a signal.'

3. 'If my unconscious mind is willing to do whatever is necessary to solve the problem, it will give a signal.'

Let's imagine you were undecided about whether you should continue as a trader. A succession of losses has eroded your confidence and your bank balance is causing serious doubts in your mind as to the wisdom of your choice of financial activity.

First you would ask your unconscious mind to give you a signal if it is willing to consider this concern of whether you should continue trading the market. You might designate the signal, such as your eyes closing, or a pulse fluttering in your neck, or a deepening of your breathing.

Alternatively, you might let the unconscious mind provide a signal for you. Say you felt a sense of excitement in your chest. You would ask for this to be repeated if it was the 'yes' signal. You might also like to set up the 'no' signal, too, although this will usually be the reverse of the 'yes' signal. That is, your eyes will remain open, you will not feel the pulse fluttering in your throat, your breathing will remain unchanged, or there will be no sense of excitement in your chest.

What if you get a 'no'?

Sometimes you do get a 'no' and at such times you must be patient. Do something else and then, say half an hour later, try again.

Do not go on to the second step until you have a 'yes' answer to the first question of whether your unconscious mind is willing to consider the issue you are raising.

Assuming you get this agreement, you would then ask your unconscious mind to explore the reason or reasons why you have been trading unsuccessfully and to give you another signal when it has done so.

There is often a very quick response to this request, though on some occasions you may have to wait patiently for some time. This is not a process to be hurried so take your time over it, adopting the detached role of an interested onlooker.

Once you get this second signal, ask your unconscious mind whether it is willing to do everything that is necessary for you to be financially successful in trading the markets. If you get no such signal, modify your question.

Ask it, for example, if it is willing to improve your proportion of winning trades gradually. You may reformulate the question a number of times, but if you get no positive response ask your unconscious mind whether it believes you should cease trading the financial markets. Perhaps this is the message, however unwelcome, that you get, and it is advice you would do well to heed.

THE 'PROCESS INSTRUCTIONS' TECHNIQUE

We tend to concentrate on a specific goal and devote relatively little attention to the procedure involved in attaining this goal.

It is often more successful to specify how people might achieve their goals and leave the 'what' ambiguous. This takes the form of using a set of content-free instructions which say 'learn something; change now'. Thus, the individual is given, very clearly, the process he or she is to go through in order to solve his or her problem, but is left very vague about any particular content which might be involved in such a solution.

The 'process instructions' approach assumes that our unconscious minds contain resources which, when effectively mobilised, will enable us to solve our problems and to change in any way we want. This effective mobilisation is achieved by talking to the unconscious rather than the conscious mind and asking it to do whatever is necessary to achieve the desired outcomes.

Don's story

This technique I used many years ago with Don, a floor trader on the verge of a nervous breakdown.

A relatively young man at 29, Don had experienced a nervous breakdown several years earlier. The experience, with its symptoms of inability to get out of bed in the morning, frequent fits of crying, black depression, and a virtual paralysis of will, had been so frightening that he was terrified of it happening again.

However, he was observing the same early-warning signals as had been present on the previous occasion – a decline in concentration, increased irritability, sleeping poorly, and consuming more alcohol.

Floor trading is a high-pressure activity and Don was showing all the signs of extreme stress. Yet, many times in the past, Don had handled such stress without any great problem. Obviously, he had the resources within himself to do so again, but he needed a way of reminding himself of this; a way of tapping into those resources again.

I established the conditions under which Don could drift into a relaxed state. This he did by focusing on his breathing, letting his out-breath carry all tightness from his body, and allowing his mind to drift in the direction of a pleasant memory.

As he did so, resting comfortably with his mind at peace, I told Don he would be able to enter the stillness of his inner mind, finding himself in a place both beautiful and pleasing where he could feel himself making contact with his deepest, innermost self. This would enable him to be at one with the tremendous power of his unconscious mind, experiencing inner resources of strength which would enable him to change in any way he wished.

I did not specify what these resources were, only that he possessed within himself the power to effect the desired changes and that his unconscious mind would be able to do whatever was necessary to select the appropriate resources.

I compared Don's unconscious mind to a computer containing in its memory everything that had ever happened to him in his entire life. From this memory, his unconscious mind would locate a very important success experience, an occasion on which he handled stress and pressure superbly well. This experience from his past life would be studied thoroughly by his unconscious mind in terms of images, sounds, and feelings. Through this thorough re-examination, Don's unconscious mind would learn what was necessary for him to reproduce, with increasing frequency, the ability to handle stress effortlessly and easily.

I made no attempt to tell Don which experience to select, when he should use the experience, or what he should use it for. These details were left to his unconscious mind. Don was simply told that he had within himself the resources he needed to be able to change and that by going through the process I have been describing, he would solve his problem.

Solve it he did. He approached his trading with renewed zest. The irritability and insomnia virtually disappearing overnight. Don possessed the ability to do this all along, rather than it being a new development. He had just forgotten the power he had, power he had used in the past to overcome stress.

I have just described the way in which I showed a trader how to improve his performance by making use of a specific technique. However, once you know how this technique works, you can use it yourself without the necessity of having someone else take you through it. The steps involved are as follows:

> - Use any of the relaxation methods outlined in this book in order to place yourself in a receptive state.
>
> - While in this state, suggest to yourself that your mind can drift back into your past and find one or more success experiences that relate to the present problem.
>
> - Suggest that your unconscious mind will study these experiences as they are vividly recreated in your imagination through pictures, sounds, and feelings. It will learn from this study everything that is necessary so that you will be able to reproduce comparable success in the future.

TATE ON TRADING

Harry has outlined some methods in this chapter that allude to the Asian concept of 'mindfulness'.

Using mindfulness, you work to detach from and watch your thoughts and feelings come and go, by staying in the present moment with a focus anchor such as your breath.

Thoughts that appear can contain incredible insights.

This is one of the reasons why Louise emphasises the importance of a Morning Journal during our Mentor Program. Louise guides the

Mentorees into creating their own Morning Journals and encourages them to write unhindered for half an hour each day, not necessarily about trading but about anything that is on their minds at any particular time.

By allowing your subconscious a voice, you minimise any potentially harmful effects, and maximise your creativity.

I'll tell you more about my views on mindfulness soon, but until then – keep reading Harry's take on how to take more control over your trading.

CHAPTER 4

TAKE MORE CONTROL OVER YOUR TRADING

'Strength does not come from winning. Your struggles develop your strengths. When you go through hardships and decide not to surrender, that is strength.'

– Arnold Schwarzenegger

THE POWER OF SELF-OBSERVATION

Every event which occurs in our lives carries with it the potential for personal growth. The process can be illustrated in the following way.

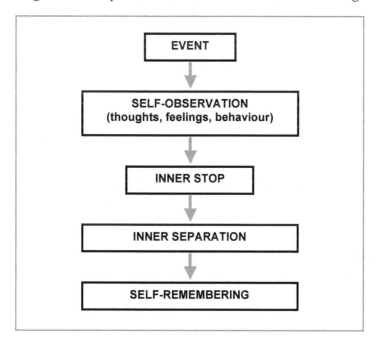

Self-observation means becoming aware of how you handle the particular event. For example, the market 'is' whereas it is you who adds the emotions of fear, hope, and greed.

BM ▷ By becoming conscious of what you are doing, you give yourself the opportunity to change this. Without such self-observation, you will mechanically repeat the same thoughts, feelings, and behaviour over and over again, even if they are very much to your disadvantage.

However, when you observe yourself doing something right, or thinking, feeling and/or behaving in a positive way, this gives you the opportunity to praise yourself. Self-praise is a far more effective approach than the usual one of looking for something we have done wrong and blaming ourselves for it.

When we observe ourselves doing something we regard as unhelpful and would prefer not to do so, we can make use of our **Inner Stop**. This is a matter of saying to ourselves, 'Stop. This is not something I want to do, or think, or feel. I do not have to put the power of my thoughts, my feelings, and my behaviour into this.'

By talking to ourselves in this way we are taking increased control over the situation by exercising our right to choose how we want to handle the event.

Through using Inner Stop, we create the opportunity to distance ourselves from the unwanted thought, feeling, or behaviour. We have employed **Inner Separation**, which involves telling ourselves, 'This is not me. I am not like this. It is not part of me.'

As Chris Tate is fond of saying: 'You are not your feelings'. This is very apt in relation to this exercise.

Self-remembering comes next as you say to yourself, 'I don't have to be like this. I can be quite different as I was when ... ', and you deliberately direct your thoughts away to some past event when you behaved, felt, or thought quite differently.

In other words, you are putting the power of your thoughts, your feelings, and your behaviour into what you choose rather than into whatever comes along.

An example

Let's see how this would work out with a particular event.

At one stage I spent three weeks in the United States. I was teaching courses on achieving change within the compass of a single therapeutic session. Other people on the teaching faculty were very pleasant and the students were so eager to learn that it was a wonderful experience, added to by the opportunity I had to dance in Waikiki both on my way to the States and on the way home.

I arrived back in Australia feeling really high, totally positive and enthusiastic. Yet virtually everyone I talked to on my return was negative, complaining about myriad trivial things. Almost without realising it, I joined in with this chorus of negativity.

Then, through self-observation, I saw what I was doing and said, 'Stop'. I then separated from the negative thoughts and feelings, and remembered how I was in the States. By immersing myself in these memories I changed my state, replacing the unwanted critical state with one of positive enthusiasm.

How does this relate to trading?

Now for a trading example.

You are trading a particular system and receive an entry signal. However, your two previous entry signals had resulted in your being stopped out at a loss on both occasions. Because of this, you talk yourself out of taking the trade.

However, if you made use of the procedure I have outlined in this chapter, you would have observed your own thoughts, feelings, and behaviour. This would have made you conscious of what you were doing.

By observing that you were talking yourself out of following your system, you give yourself the opportunity to say, 'No. I won't behave like this. If I am going to follow the system, I have to take every entry signal which accords with the rules.'

Inner Separation can then take place as you tell yourself something like, 'I am not like this, a person who lacks the discipline to follow the system, a person who vacillates and cannot carry through with the course I have set myself.' Self-Remembering then comes to the fore as you recall a trade several months ago in which you followed the system rules automatically and reaped the benefit of a big profit.

This is how the process works but it requires practice. A lot of practice.

I remind myself every morning that I am committed to operating in this way. I do this because of the enormous benefits it has brought, enabling me to take more control over my life than I ever imagined possible.

This process comes between you and life, allowing you to manage many of the events that previously managed you. Initially, you certainly won't be able to do this on every occasion. As human beings we are far from perfect so we must just do the best we can. However, if you realise that you have blindly gone ahead and done something without observing yourself in the manner I have outlined, all is not lost. In your imagination, go back over the event, this time doing it correctly by observing yourself and your reactions to the events, stopping the negatives, separating from them, and remembering a positive event.

TURN YOUR ADDICTIONS INTO PREFERENCES

When we are asked about our addictions, what springs to mind most readily would be activities such as smoking, eating chocolate, and drinking alcohol. Another way of considering this term, however, relates more closely to the concept of emotional control. In order to find out what you are addicted to, use your anger as a signal, for this is telling you that someone or something is not living up to your expectations.

Len's story

Len was able to do this very successfully. Slippage really annoyed Len. He would become very angry when he found that an entry or an exit order had been filled at a price different from the one he had anticipated. He could have used limit rather than market orders, but preferred, particularly with his exits, to use the latter.

His anger over poor fills, which was usually quite out of proportion to the situation, interfered with the dispassionate, detached view of the market that he wished to cultivate.

Len's anger was saying that he was addicted to getting his market orders filled at the price he anticipated. Though we would all like this desirable result, experience has taught us that it is more of a hope rather than a reasonable expectation.

It is a matter of expectations. All of us, at times, impose expectations (just as unrealistic as demanding perfect fills) on people around us – and become very upset when we don't get the result we want.

What Len was really saying to himself is: 'My order <u>must</u> be filled at the best possible price. If it isn't, I just can't stand it.' Totally unrealistic of course, but it seems that human beings do think in this irrational manner as they try to change the world to suit themselves.

This is just not going to happen. The world is not going to change because we want it to. Our choice is either to continue to be angry when our expectations are not met, or to modify them so they become more reasonable.

Unless we wish to react automatically with anger every time our expectations are not met, we need to transform our addictions into preferences. Turning Len's addiction – that his orders should always be filled well – into a 'preference' would be ideal. This outcome would help Len achieve the emotional discipline that is the mark of the good trader. He could choose to make this transformation along the following lines:

> I would prefer it if my orders were filled at the best possible price but it is highly unlikely, given the nature of markets, that this will always happen.
>
> Instead of fuming about what I regard as poor fills, I'd be better off accepting this as an inevitable part of trading. After all, I do get some good fills, sometimes better than expected, and I do make profitable trades despite bad fills.
>
> It is not as if I actually achieve anything by my anger other than making myself feel bad. It doesn't change anything and doesn't help me get better fills in the future, so I'm achieving nothing positive.
>
> What I've been doing in the past is becoming highly emotional, possibly damaging my health by the fierceness of my reaction, and interfering with the rationality of my decision-making. This can only have a negative influence on my ability to trade profitably.

Len won't achieve this transformation overnight, but with constant practice it will be possible for him to gain greatly increased control over his emotions, improving both his health and his trading.

OTHER PATHS TO INCREASED EMOTIONAL DISCIPLINE

It is because trading tends to attract people who are ill-suited to the task that the need for emotional discipline must be emphasised so strongly. Many of those embarking upon trading are driven by the power of one goal only: to make vast amounts of money. Others are risk takers, needing a constant adrenalin rush to enjoy their lives. These people seek the excitement of the market and react to the world with great emotional intensity.

If individuals of this ilk are to achieve any success, they will need to back off somewhat so they can place some distance between the market and themselves. Perhaps they could take a leaf out of the book of the mothers-to-be with whom I work. One of the techniques I teach them is to separate from their bodies so that, from the ceiling or the other side of the room, they can watch themselves having their baby. Once their baby is born, they get back 'inside themselves' again to enjoy the closeness without having had to experience the pain. Not all can achieve this state completely but many do. In fact, many sportspeople have this type of experience when 'playing out of their minds', as do those who have been clinically dead and then recovered.

I know that Louise implemented this method very successfully with the birth of both of her children.

This separation of mind and body requires considerable practice but, for you as a trader, you would mentally 'see' yourself from a distance, sitting in your chair, working on your charts virtually as if you were watching another person. You would be viewing yourself from the outside, completely detached. Some people who use this approach describe it as if they were watching a movie of themselves in action, but one in which they are not really involved.

What you are doing here is changing the way your brain perceives the trading situation. Once you have done this, you change the manner in which it will respond to that situation forever. It is as if you are now an observer of yourself and, in times of stress, this is invaluable.

In his interview with Jack Schwager in *The New Market Wizards*, Tom Basso described how he used this technique when talking to groups of people, an activity which caused him considerable anxiety. When he found himself shaking in this situation, his observer would say:

> 'Why are you shaking Tom? Just relax. You're talking too fast. Slow down a little bit.'

Sounds too simple to work – but it does!

Eventually your observer can be there all the time if this is what would be useful to you. Once you develop this skill it is similar to watching a movie. You see yourself playing a part in this movie called 'Life'.

You may not want to take it to these lengths but it is of inestimable value in pressure situations such as trading as you say to yourself: 'I'm going to watch myself do this trade'.

TO STOP OR NOT TO STOP

Emotional detachment is very valuable when the use of stops is considered. It is clear that we know more than we think we know. Accessing our unconscious minds can put us in touch with this previously unused information. However, conversely, we often have the knowledge we need but we don't use it. Using stops is a case in point.

Virtually every successful trader uses stops in one form or another. Every worthwhile book on money management, while acknowledging that stops don't always do the job they are supposed to do, emphasises their importance if you are to survive as a trader. Yet often we do not use them. Why not?

For one thing, their use is not very rewarding. In most cases, a stop will get you out with a loss or a smaller profit than you had.

There is nothing positive about stops, other than the avoidance of a loss.

Every time a stop is hit you may feel as if you have been punished. Why should you continue to use stops when what they bring is punishment? This is what accounts for the hesitation that many traders experience in taking losses.

Stops are clearly important for money-management purposes. The question is, then, how can we find some positive aspect to their use that will change our attitude towards them? My advice is to keep a record of what you save yourself through the use of stops. Each time your stop saves you from a greater loss or a lesser profit, reward yourself immediately.

I know that Louise has implemented this concept very well, in conjunction with her system tester – Scott Lowther. Scott began to track the progression of Louise's trades, after she had exited her positions. It became clear that stops prevented future losses in almost every situation.

LOUISE'S THOUGHTS

You've hit a critical part of Harry's book. Either you're starting to let Harry's words wash over you and enter your trading soul, or … you're starting to reject his views. Sometimes people are quick to reject if they've been hurt in the past. The market can kick us like a mule, but it's up to us whether we get up off the floor to give it another shot.

I urge you to keep an open mind.

Effective learning is error-driven. Failures grab our attention.

In fact, researchers have found that the more wildly wrong our predictions are about the markets, the more quickly we learn. Our brain needs failure to create success.

As Bruce Kovner states in the terrific book *Market Wizards*: 'You have to be willing to make mistakes regularly; there is nothing wrong with it. Michael [Marcus] taught me about making your best judgment, being wrong, making your next best judgment, being wrong, making your third best judgment, and then doubling your money.'

Failing with flair boils down to three aspects. It involves controlling our emotions, adjusting our thinking, and re-evaluating our beliefs about ourselves.

According to Yale psychologist Susan Nolen-Hoeksema, the real difference between people who manage to snatch victory from the jaws of defeat and those who slip into a self-defeating abyss involves one key factor: people who ultimately succeed nip 'rumination' in the bud. Rather than continuing to be so self-involved with morbid, spiralling self-talk, they turn the corner and focus on what they can learn from the lesson. They force themselves to move on and set a goal for the future. This is essential advice for all traders who have faced a drawdown in their trading careers.

So if you're feeling like a failure, I have an insight for you. As Philip Schultz, author of *Failure*, states: 'Everyone thinks they're a failure. The only people who don't are the ones who really are.'

Next time you take a hit in the markets, refuse to dwell on it, and just realise you're one step closer to your next successful trade. Learn from the experience and move on.

Harry's about to tell you the sporting arena can help you to trade well. Keep reading now to hear his take on it …

CHAPTER 5

TRADING AS A SPORT

'Change your thoughts and you change your world.'

– Norman Vincent Peale

Similarities abound between trading and playing a sport. Luckily, many of the techniques which have enabled athletes to perform more effectively can be used to enhance trading performance. Plus, many people can relate more easily to sporting examples than to those associated with trading – so let's begin by considering some typical sporting situations.

SOME SPORTING EXAMPLES

Margaret is a tennis player who seems unable to beat a certain opponent. She loses to her six times in succession, then wins after recovering from a position of apparently certain defeat.

She never loses to that player again.

Compare this situation to that of the trader who cannot seem to make more than a certain amount of money. Every time she exceeds this amount, she embarks on a series of losing trades. The result – she has to start over again. Then, just once, she makes a real killing. More importantly, she is able to maintain this profit level, which is well above her previous limit amount.

Like Margaret, who, when she exceeded her previous limit of losing, was able to continue performing at a higher level, so too can this trader.

Once the self-imposed ceiling is breached, it usually ceases to have any further limiting power.

Gary is a golfer who expects to miss putts. When he lines up a putt, he 'knows' he will miss most of the time. Is Gary so dissimilar from traders who expect to lose? They are victims of the market, believing the fates are unkind and punishing so that no matter what they do, it will go wrong.

Why do things like this happen in sport, in trading, and in every aspect of life?

Perhaps the concept of the Inner Game can provide an explanation.

WHAT IS THE INNER GAME?

Playing sport is all about winning, about beating your opponents and enhancing your reputation by doing so. Or is it?

There is another way of looking at sport which has, for many participants, brought more satisfaction than the 'winning is all' attitude. This alternative view has been developed by Tim Gallwey in his books *The Inner Game of Tennis* and *Inner Tennis*.

Though he uses tennis to illustrate his ideas, the concept is applicable to any sport, to trading, and to the game of life itself.

As Gallwey explains it, in any sport there are two games involved. The first of these, the Outer Game, pits us against obstacles presented by external opponents, and provides external prizes such as trophies, money, and reputation.

The second, the Inner Game, is played against internal mental and emotional obstacles for the reward of increased self-realisation. Every human activity, Gallwey believes, involves both external and internal barriers. There are many sources for the former. However, for the latter, there is but one source, the mind, which is easily distracted by its tendency to worry, agonise and become upset.

A basketball player misses several shots. His shooting becomes increasingly tentative and, as a result, his accuracy deteriorates. He talks to himself in negative ways, telling himself he is a poor shooter. This virtually ensures he will continue missing. His self-talk moves from the concept of himself as a poor shooter to that of being an inadequate basketball player.

In turn, his inferior performance can plunge him into such misery and despair that self-doubt about his value as a person results. Though, initially, you may feel this is an exaggeration, I am sure you will agree that you have reacted in a similar way over some equally trivial event, catastrophising and expanding it out of all proportion to its actual importance.

Trader Tom

Consider how we could apply this concept to a trader, Tom.

Tom continually attempts, with little success, to pick tops and bottoms. Every time his analysis suggests that a top or a bottom has occurred, he loses money, and he berates himself for his poor chart analysis.

After behaving in this way on a number of occasions he begins doubting his ability to analyse his charts and tells himself he is a hopeless technical trader. Such negative self-statements make him feel badly about himself, miserable, and depressed, because being a successful trader is an ego issue with him. He should be able to trade successfully. After all, isn't he a very prosperous businessman, accustomed to making profitable decisions? Therefore, he also should be able to analyse a chart to the point where the market performs in accordance with his prediction.

When it doesn't, it is a blow to his self-esteem and, should this be a frequent occurrence, he will begin to doubt his ability, first as a trader, then as a capable person.

If, however, Tom was a practitioner of the Inner Game, he would behave differently. By observing his thoughts and watching his reactions in an uninvolved manner, he would be able to see that the problem is in his mind rather than in the external event itself. He would realise that he was creating pressure upon himself through his imagined beliefs about the harm of a particular event, such as making errors in his technical analysis.

Instead of creating his self-imposed pressure, Tom would do better to practise a detached awareness of the present. He could observe what is happening without attempting to evaluate it as good, bad, or indifferent.

The Inner Game involves using our inner resources so that we can become as good as we are capable of being. It is not a matter of adding qualities to a self that we see as being deficient in some way, but of freeing ourselves from whatever is preventing us from realising our full potential.

We cannot, for example, acquire accuracy in technical analysis if we assume it isn't already there. However, what we can do is to encourage the expression and development of improved chart analysis, or any other quality, which we accept as already existing within us, at least to some degree.

This is possible if we rid ourselves of the limitations we have created in our own mind.

Our inner obstacles

The essence of the Inner Game, then, lies in overcoming the mental obstacles that prevent us from attaining our goals. There are many such obstacles, one of the most powerful being fear. The fear of losing or of making errors will often cause us to become tense under pressure so that we make mistakes. The fear of looking bad in the eyes of others, or of not meeting expectations, both our own and others, will have a similar result.

So, too, will other inner obstacles such as the lack of concentration due to mind wandering, the absence of determination resulting in the reluctance to take valid entry signals, and the self-consciousness that finds us constantly thinking about how well or badly we are trading. All of these make it difficult to trade as well as we are capable of trading.

In turn, other mental barriers make their appearance. Frustration is one of the more common, as is the anger that comes after making simple mistakes. Such anger may be directed at ourselves, the market, our bad luck, or unanticipated world events, but it is often self-doubt or a general lack of self-confidence that underlies these emotional outbursts.

This can be the most damaging of all internal obstacles. Without a belief in ourselves and our abilities we are unlikely to be winners. This is particularly so if we indulge in self-condemnation, blaming ourselves for being less than perfect.

Perfection is unattainable, for – being human – we are not perfect, and are most unlikely to ever be so. Yet, if we refuse to let ourselves feel good until we achieve perfection, we are going to be constantly unhappy. This is always the case when we set ourselves a goal that is incapable of achievement.

Often what happens when we have such a goal is that we try too hard, constantly evaluating our performance in negative terms. Overcoming this need to evaluate, and overcoming the other barriers mentioned above, is the key skill of the Inner Game, one that involves increasing our awareness of what is actually happening in our immediate experience.

Awareness

We first encounter the Inner Game when we realise that there is an opponent within our own heads who is far more formidable than the ones provided by the outside world. This opponent prevents us from performing at our best and also prevents us from living our best lives. A mind disturbed by anxiety, self-doubt, and concern about our image, and, as a result, filled with internal instructions and self-criticisms, is most unlikely to facilitate the full expression of our potential.

Players of the Inner Game know that the errors they make in their trading performance usually take place in their minds before they actually occur in their actions. They know that the only real obstacles in trading are those they impose upon themselves. Removal of these will allow them to enjoy and express their true capabilities.

Trusting your unconscious mind is an essential ingredient of the Inner Game. Your capacity to learn without the help of verbal self-instructions from the conscious mind is much greater than you imagine. It is only when you succeed in quieting the conscious mind that your true potential can begin to show itself. That is why it is important to 'let things happen'.

The Inner Game approach suggests that, if you want to change your trading performance, or your life, do not deliberately try to change it. Simply increase your non-judgemental awareness of the way things actually are at the moment.

Gallwey argues that your calm acceptance of an undesired action is more likely to decrease the chance of it recurring than if you fight against it, evaluating it as bad. Such behaviour will usually increase a habit's frequency. This is why Gallwey emphasises the importance of increasing your awareness of the events in your experience without imposing upon them the concepts of 'good' and 'bad'.

If, after a careful analysis of current data on a particular commodity, you take a position the timing of which is all wrong, it is counter-productive to label your action as 'bad'. It is far more important to see exactly what occurred. If you simply make the evaluation of 'bad', you are unlikely to notice the details upon which you based your trading decision. Consequently you do not give your unconscious mind the accurate feedback it requires in order to make corrections the next time you are faced with a similar decision.

You're only human

Being imperfect, we are going to make mistakes in whatever we do in life. However, it is not as important to eliminate these occasional mistakes as it is to rid ourselves of the fear of making errors, and of the sense of failure we are prone to attach to them.

Unfortunately, we are conditioned to believe that improvement is a result of telling ourselves what is wrong and what is right. If we can bring ourselves to quieten this flow of instructions, we will find that awareness alone is usually capable of bringing about the desired changes in our trading performance or in our behaviour in general.

This awareness approach, rather than the evaluation approach, is applicable to virtually all of life's situations.

Handling pain

To handle physical pain, it is necessary to increase your awareness of it, focusing your attention on your body so that you can locate the source of the pain quite precisely.

What kind of pain is it? Would you describe it in terms of a strain, tension, ache, or sharp twinge? Where exactly does it occur? On a scale of 1 to 10, decide how much it hurts when you perform certain actions such as turning, bending, or stretching.

Don't try to avoid the pain or correct for it in any way. Instead, continue to discriminate the degree of hurt on succeeding movements by grading it on the 10-point scale.

By simply experiencing it and objectively observing how it increases or decreases with each movement, you will gain increased control over your pain, reducing its effect upon you. You can then change the physical properties you have given it and so change the pain itself.

Having recently been through a major heart operation, I can attest to the benefits of this method.

Julia's story

Using this method is how Julia, a hairdresser who had been trading part-time for several years, handled an ache in her neck. The ache had developed as a result both of her work and of the angle at which she had been holding her head while looking at charts on her computer. She had taken steps to rectify the situation both in the hairdressing salon and the room where she had her computer but, despite medical assistance, the pain continued.

I had Julia describe the pain, which she located at a particular point in her neck. She experienced it as red, heavy, hot, circular in shape, and quite large.

She was able to change its colour to a pleasant green, cool it with an imaginary fan, compress it into a cube, and throw it out the window. As she did so, her face and body reflected the change that was taking place within her.

She confirmed that the pain had disappeared and, during a follow-up discussion six months later, stated that it had returned on two occasions only. In both these cases, she was able to remove it virtually instantly by identifying its physical characteristics and changing these. In this way she had taken control over the pain.

To gain increased awareness of our body, we need to relax conscious control over our actions, something that is not all that easy to accomplish. We seem to think we must exert conscious control over what we are doing or we will not be able to do it. However, shifting control from the conscious to the unconscious mind is the essence of playing the Inner Game.

Winners and losers

It is through playing against the opponent in your mind that you come to an increased knowledge of your true potential, and it is the market, your external opponent, that provides you with the opportunity to play this Inner Game.

Whether your external opponent wins or not is irrelevant, for you are still able to triumph against your inner opponent by overcoming the obstacles thrown up by your own mind. Every trade you make is one more opportunity to improve your Inner Game.

External circumstances can prevent us from winning the outer rewards, but only we can prevent ourselves from achieving the internal ones. Though the market may deprive us of external victory, it cannot prevent us from being victorious over our own minds. Therein lies a tremendous advantage for Inner Game players. The goal of trying to attain our full potential is entirely within our own control, for no external event can prevent us from exerting our maximum effort.

Because you – as a player of the Inner Game – possess this control, you cannot be denied the benefits of your efforts. Thus you will feel no anxiety.

Self-esteem

The Inner Game can, however, provide a more substantial basis for self-esteem. Look upon the opponent in your head as your main problem. The mental obstacles it generates prevent you from living your best life. This means that the only real obstacles in life are ones you impose on yourself.

Removing them allows you to become the person you are capable of being. You will be able to express your true capabilities free of fear, self-doubt, self-condemnation, poor concentration, perfectionism, frustration, anger, boredom, and all the other self-created 'mind problems'.

So you have choices. You may choose to play the Inner Game in order to reach an outer goal. Conversely, you may prefer to play the Outer Games to help you reach inner goals.

TATE ON TRADING

I was channel-hopping the other night when I came across one of those reality shows that now seem to make up some 90 per cent of all shows on TV – and which bear no resemblance to reality whatsoever. (Unfortunately no-one has taken me up on my idea for a reality show called *Celebrity Bomb Disposal* and its spin-off *Celebrity Mine Clearance*. However, that is another story.)

This show revolved around a hedge fund manager stumping up some of his money to a series of hopefuls. I originally thought, 'Damn – that is gutsy'. However, I then thought about the range of talent that has emerged from our Mentor Program and thought – perhaps not.

The interesting thing about this show was, from what I could tell, their training consisted of two weeks on how to operate the dealing program with no instruction on trading itself. So it really was a 'sink or swim' proposition.

This is not such an unusual position for the newbie trader to find themselves in. The typical evolution of a trader goes something like this. You have read a few magazines, perhaps bought a few shares, you may even have seen *Wall Street* on video. You go to bed Sunday night all a jitter with your perceived new-found expertise, wake up Monday morning and decide that you are a stock market trader.

Not too implausible you think? After all, you have probably been able to master a few skills in your life, why not trading?

Well, consider a variation on the theme. Imagine that you have seen a few episodes of *ER*, perhaps you have even been to the doctor once or twice. On the basis of this background you decide that you are more than adequately qualified to be a trauma surgeon. So you nip down to the local hospital and offer your services.

Sounds silly, but it's no sillier than deciding to trade the stock market without actually having any background as a trader.

You may consider yourself a trader on the basis that you have made a little bit of money when the market has been running hard. But consider carefully the following questions, which are arranged in order of importance, and see if you can answer them:

- What is your position-sizing algorithm? Is it based upon percentage give back, volatility, or a technical tool?

- What is your exit trigger, more commonly known as a stop loss?

- What is your entry system?

These are some of the most basic of questions that all professional traders simply take for granted. If you cannot answer these questions then you should acknowledge that you do not know anything about the basics of trading.

If you have made any money in any market and you cannot answer these three questions then you have been lucky.

Yes, lucky.

You have displayed no more skill than someone who wins the lottery.

To develop your trading mindset further, you will want to get the CD set that I made in conjunction with Louise and Harry called *Psychology Secrets* (from www.tradinggame.com.au). We take you through the ten most common trading mistakes as well as practical solutions you can implement immediately.

Work on yourself and your trading plan as hard as if you were studying to be a surgeon. Only then will you get the results in the markets you crave.

Next, Harry's going to talk about the key aspects of superior performance. So keep reading to find out what they are and how you can benefit ...

CHAPTER 6

KEY ASPECTS OF SUPERIOR PERFORMANCE

'Your time is limited, don't waste it living someone else's life. Don't let the noise of other's opinion drown your own inner voice. Have the courage to follow your heart and intuition, they somehow already know what you truly want to become.'

– Steve Jobs

Over a wide range of endeavours, including trading, six key factors consistently separate the winners from the losers.

1. SELF-BELIEF

NEGATIVE AND POSITIVE SELF-TALK	
Negative	**Positive**
You are a fool. How could you have made that trade?	Everyone makes mistakes. Concentrate on the next trade.
What will (X) think of me now?	I'm doing my best. The good trades will take care of themselves.
I hope I don't make a terrible trade like that again.	
Those floor traders picked me off again.	Relax, exercise discipline, and make your next trade.
	I have to think more critically about where to place my stops.

It is important to talk to yourself in ways that will enhance, rather than inhibit, your performance. It would appear as if your mind, or the subconscious part of it, operates much like a computer in that it accepts uncritically whatever program is fed into it. If you tell yourself you are capable of winning you have far more chance of achieving that outcome than if you tell yourself that you are going to lose.

To demonstrate to yourself just how powerfully your attitudes are influenced by the words you use, choose some aspect of your life towards which you know your mental attitude could be improved. Keeping this in mind, write down these areas of mental attitude improvement.

I have listed five such sentences to illustrate the type of responses you could give in relation to trading:

> 'It's difficult for me to ensure that I place a stop with every trade.'

> 'I hope that I can do the work that will enable me to become an exceptional trader.'

> 'If I really stick to the rules of my proven system, then I will become a winner.'

> 'I'm going to try to learn all I can about being a successful trader.'

> 'I can't "pull the trigger".'

When you have done this, take a moment to consider what you have written. Notice how the sentences reflect your attitude about the situation. Now rewrite the sentences, amending the first few words as follows:

> Replace 'It's difficult for me to …' with 'It's a challenge for me to …'

> Replace 'I hope that …' with 'I know that …'

> Replace 'If I … then …' with 'When I … then …'

> Replace 'I'm going to try to …' with 'I'm going to …'

> Replace 'I can't …' with 'I won't …'

Do you see how the second version releases new energy into the situation you describe and suggests a new way of looking at it?

Resolve to make these changes when you speak about yourself in future, consciously interrupting your own negative language and replacing it with positive language.

Just positive thinking?

This proposition may be dismissed as 'just positive thinking'.

It is true that positive thinking has its limitations, although this is usually a fault of the way it is employed. The positive thinking in which we are usually urged to engage is more realistically described as wishful thinking. It is unlikely to help us improve our performance. Due to its focus on goals such as 'I will win' or 'This trade has everything going for it', it is of no assistance in guiding us to do whatever is needed to achieve these outcomes.

No information is given about what actions we need to take.

With 'wishful thinking', all you may achieve when you talk positively to yourself – saying things like 'I must make a profit on this trade' – is to remind yourself that the reverse might come true.

If I said to you not to think of a pink elephant, you would immediately think of this somewhat unusual animal. This is due to the fact that before you can 'not think' of it, you have to think of it. So attempting to cheer up a friend by telling him or her not to worry is unlikely to be at all helpful. Quite the contrary. Before your friend can 'stop worrying', he or she has to start and continue to worry, a situation you do not want to occur.

An alternative to wishful thinking is to use unhelpful thoughts as cues or triggers to generate thoughts more likely to assist your performance. As the trader studies his computer screen, he might find he is talking to himself in a way likely to cause an error. He tells himself that it is a difficult market, that the daily newspaper carried an article advising behaviour quite different from that which he is contemplating, and that his last trade in this contract resulted in a loss. All of these comments are likely to interfere with the detached, analytical approach needed to make a sound decision. However, he could use this negative self-talk as a cue to pull himself up short and deliberately switch into a productive, positive-thinking mode. This he could do by reminding himself that the particular pattern that he is observing on his computer screen has, in the past, produced consistent profits and that it is usually a successful move to trade, contrary to the views expressed in the daily press.

This is a matter of coupling the imagination of what you desire – not what you fear – with positive internal-success dialogue. So, instead of attempting to keep negative thoughts out of your mind, welcome them as cues – triggers that generate positive thoughts, images, and dialogue about yourself and your performance.

2. TOTAL CONCENTRATION AND FOCUS DURING COMPETITION

Total concentration and focus is the second aspect of superior performance.

As well as generating positive thoughts, cues can be very useful in helping you focus your attention. As far as sport is concerned, this process can begin in the dressing room as you prepare for battle. While taking off your street clothes, imagine you are also taking off fear, self-doubt, and indecision. As you put on the clothes you wear to play your sport, imagine you are putting on confidence, self-assurance, strength, and concentration. A final action, tightening your shoelaces, can be felt as tightening up your determination to the point where you feel nothing can stop your success.

To some extent this same procedure may be followed by a trader who may prepare him or herself for the analysis of charts by putting on a favourite jacket, sitting in a special 'trading' chair, and working in a special 'trading' area.

As sportspeople move out onto the playing area, they can make use of cues in the environment. Volleyball players can, for example, concentrate on the lines on the court, narrowing the focus of their attention until nothing exists for them except the area within these lines.

Similarly the trader could focus firstly on the door to the room in which he or she keeps charts, then to the desk, then narrowing the concentration area further to focus on the charts or the computer screen. Use of such cues helps you narrow both your visual attention and your mental concentration.

The bubble technique

As a further aid to concentration, the trader could follow the lead of Julie, a part-time trader who constructs a 'bubble' around herself. This 'bubble' is like the cone of silence so beloved in spy stories where the protagonists meet in a room in which there is a cage made of special, totally sound-proofed glass. Nothing can be heard through this glass.

Each of us can use our imagination to create such an environment for ourselves.

In Julie's case, her 'concentration bubble' not only blocks out all sound but it also blocks out visual distractions. She has made it opaque so that nothing can be seen through it. When Julie goes into her 'concentration bubble', nothing distracts her.

She is free to concentrate totally on the task at hand, that of studying her charts and making trading decisions. Should she think of something that she needs to do, rather than allowing this to disturb her concentration, she notes it on her 'distraction pad', together with a specific time at which she will attend to this task. When that time arrives, she stops work on her trading materials, removes her 'concentration bubble', and attends to the various items that have occurred to her while she was working.

The idea of a fresh start is valuable too. The golfer can approach each shot as if it were the first one in the round. If the previous shot has been bungled, this is immaterial. The present one is all that matters.

So, too, with trading. Each trade is a separate entity in itself, totally independent of those that have preceded it. Irrespective of whether previous trades have produced profits or losses, the present trade stands on its own feet and is a fresh beginning; the first trade in the trader's career.

3. VISUALISATION OF YOUR PERFORMANCE BEFORE THE EVENT

The third key factor of superior performance is to remember your very best performances, the 'magic moments' when everything went right for you. Use all your senses to invoke these as vividly as possible – what you would have seen, heard, felt, smelt, and tasted in the situation. Link these together as a continuous mental video tape of masterly performance, with one success experience blending into the next. Then, transpose these to the future, visualising yourself doing the same things in the setting of this performance. Make this as vivid as possible.

The split-screen technique is a good way of channelling visualisations to enhance their power. Visualise a large screen which is divided into three segments. Initially, the screen is black but, to begin the procedure, imagine the right-hand segment becoming illuminated with a picture of yourself in your present state. This might involve a picture of yourself in a situation where your lack of confidence is exercising a negative effect on your self-esteem. Perhaps you might see yourself receiving the signal to take a trade but failing to place your order, or allowing yourself to be unduly influenced by your broker.

Remove this picture, allowing the right-hand segment of the screen to go dark. The centre segment then lights up as you visualise yourself receiving some form of assistance, such as attending a seminar on trading methodology, which will help you change this unconfident behaviour. You might imagine yourself in the room where you experienced the technique, 'seeing' yourself, the group leader, and the surroundings.

The centre of the screen then goes dark as you activate the left-hand segment with a picture of yourself as you would like to be. In this picture you are confident, handling the previously mismanaged situation with ease and aplomb so that you achieve the results you desire from the interaction.

This split-screen concept, with movement from the right of the screen reflecting the past to the left of the screen reflecting the future, is derived from De Silva's Mind Control technique.

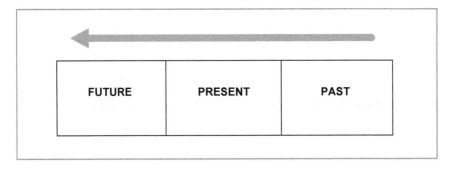

The Time Line method

Another alternative visualisation approach, the Time Line, indicates that, for many people, their future is to the right and their past to the left. Others have their past behind them and their future in front of them. Experimentation will be needed to find which of these patterns seems to suit you best. Use it with the basic concept of first 'seeing' the past, then the present, and finally the future.

Some people – such as athletes, musicians, and public speakers – mentally prepare themselves in this way for weeks before a performance. Others become bored doing this, so they use the approach over a more limited time span of a few days, or even only the evening before.

Most successful performers do make use of their powers of visualisation in one form or another. This is true even of people who supposedly do not have the ability to 'see pictures in their minds'. If these people are asked to describe what such pictures would be like if they were able to 'see' them, they are usually able to do so quite successfully. So they actually can use visualisation even though they previously may have thought they were unable to do so.

After all, the point of power is our minds because thoughts can be manipulated. Unfortunately most people do so to their detriment, filling their minds with what they fear, what they do not want, instead of with what they desire.

The market is only a thought in your mind. If the way you choose to think about the market generates fear and anxiety, it would seem sensible to change this thought and, by so doing, change your perception of the market. Instead of the negatives in your mind, replace them with symbols of success and power.

The pyramid technique

One particularly effective technique that will help you to feel confident in your ability to achieve involves using a pyramid as a visualisation object. Imagine yourself back in ancient Egypt, standing in the desert before the cave-like entrance to a large pyramid. As you enter, you find yourself in a downward-sloping passageway, well lit by torches. Feeling a sense of security and confidence, you follow this passageway as it takes you deeper and deeper into the heart of the pyramid.

At the very end of the passage is a vast storeroom filled with treasures of all descriptions. This is the storehouse of all the vast untapped resources – all the potential for good and for achievement – which you have not yet turned to your advantage. All of this treasure is rightfully yours, for it has been stolen from you through force of circumstance. However, unless you carry it back into the world outside to enjoy and to share with others, it will eventually be sealed up within the room and lost forever.

Naturally, you attempt to gather your treasure. Yet, you cannot. Some force is preventing you, a force emanating from a huge black statue in the centre of the room. This statue, powered by a brilliant jewel embedded in its forehead, is the embodiment of all the negative forces of failure and defeat within you. It has been placed in the room as the guardian of the treasure, making all other guardians unnecessary.

To free this vast storehouse of your potential so that you can become the person you are capable of being, you must first overcome the negative tendencies; the forces of failure and defeat within you that are acting to prevent this, these tendencies being personified and embodied in the guardian statue.

Go to the statue and knock the jewel from its forehead. As it lies on the ground, its lustre fades, so that it looks dark and ugly like a piece of coal. This can be stepped upon and crushed into black dust. Its power gone, the statue may then be pushed so that it falls and breaks into many pieces.

You are now free to gather as much of the treasure as can be carried, taking it with you as you retrace your steps up the passage to the entrance. There is no need to attempt to take all the treasure, for you will be able to return to this treasure room whenever you want to. No matter how much you may take, or how many times you return, the room will never be empty.

Step outside into the warm sunshine, and return to the world of your everyday life with the treasures you have gathered. These treasures, which can be anything you want them to be, will reveal themselves in new habits, new ideas, and new directions.

On any occasion when you feel a lack of confidence in your ability to do something, think of the pyramid and the treasures it contains while, at the same time, using a physical signal such as clenching the fist of your dominant hand. As you do these two things, you will feel a sense of confidence, strength, and power surging through you, filling you with the certainty that you are capable of accomplishing the task about which you were doubtful.

Followers of NLP (Neuro-Linguistic Programming) will recognise this concept as the basis of 'anchoring'.

4. ANALYSING TRADES TO IMPROVE PERFORMANCE AND STRATEGY

The fourth key aspect of superior performance involves using your mind to make performance as good as it is capable of being. At the end of each day, spend a few minutes recalling what you have done, particularly those things related to your trading activity.

Think of the things you did well, running each one through your mind half a dozen times and congratulating yourself on these. We are very reluctant to praise ourselves compared with the ease with which we indulge in self-criticism. It is helpful to redress this imbalance.

Possibly the most powerful technique to bring out the best in other people is to catch them doing something right and praise them for it. This is in marked contrast to what we usually do, which is to catch people doing something wrong and blame them for it (keeping silent when they are doing the right thing). Don't be like this with yourself.

Be supportive and encouraging. Go back over your performance, pick out the things you did well, visualise yourself doing them again several times, then praise yourself for what you have done. In other words, behave as if you were your own best friend, being supportive and encouraging.

After this brief review of the day's positive aspects, take some time to consider your mistakes. One at a time, wipe each one from your mind the way you would wipe chalk off a chalkboard, and replay it mentally five or six times the way you wish you had performed in that situation. In the sporting context, this would mean that if you missed the easy putt, 'see yourself' sinking that putt successfully five or six times. When applied to trading, this procedure would have you identifying errors of analysis, ignoring trades signalled by your system because of 'expert' advice, placing a stop carelessly, or exiting a trade too soon. Do this for each of your main errors, then mentally leave that day's events.

The day is over.

Look forward to what lies ahead.

5. LETTING GO OF DEFEATS: ANTICIPATING FUTURE CHALLENGES

The fifth key aspect of superior performance involves achieving a mental shift through reframing. This is a process of placing thoughts in a different perspective so that things are seen in a different way.

Athletes replying to the question, 'What is the worst thing that could happen to me now?' frequently explode their nervousness away in laughter as they become aware of the triviality of their concerns. Things are worth what we make them worth. Unfortunately, we can make them worth too much. Tell yourself not to worry about trivialities, then remind yourself that virtually all the things you do fret about are trivialities.

The process of taking something which has been previously seen in negative terms and extracting something positive from it can be seen in the very powerful reframe: 'There is no such thing as failure, only feedback'. That is, instead of labelling something as a failure, you search for some aspect which can be construed in positive terms.

Perhaps you missed a trading opportunity through fear, or stayed too long in a trade because of greed, or refused to accept that the market was not behaving as you expected and stayed in hoping that it would turn around. Events such as this teach us a great deal about ourselves if we are prepared to listen. By identifying our greed, fear, and hope, we are more likely to avoid such pitfalls in subsequent trades, for these characteristics are a root cause of many trading failures.

Greed is the belief that there is never enough. We can reframe by accepting that the market is always there and opportunities abound. Hope encourages procrastination in a losing position, hoping the market will come back or there will be a reaction permitting a better exit point. We reframe by accepting that hope is just an idea, one that usually has little relation to reality.

The market is the reality. Accordingly, we put on a stop so that the market tells us when we are wrong and eliminates the useless hoping that things will turn out all right despite the market telling us otherwise.

Fear will cause you to stay out of a trade. It will also cause you to act impulsively. One reframe here is to be businesslike and accept losses as one aspect of doing business, rather than fearing them.

Instead of fretting about a missed opportunity, put it into perspective. Just where does it lie on the 1 to 10 scale of importance? Probably about 0.2!

By putting the 'mistake' into perspective you can turn it into a challenge to avail yourself of the next opportunity. The market is always there, continually providing opportunities for trading. Accept that sometimes you will overlook what is being offered and use this as a spur to improve your future alertness.

Formulating goals is another way of shifting your focus from past defeats to future challenges. Setting yourself a target, such as a certain percentage of winning to losing trades, or an annual profit figure, is often not productive. It has the effect of encouraging you to 'force a trade' (that is, to trade where the opportunity is not optimal). A more appropriate goal is to aim to follow your trading plan, to the letter, for 20 trades in a row.

This is useful particularly if you set up a series of sub-goals along the way. By doing this you can reward yourself with praise each time you achieve a sub-goal instead of having to wait until your main goal has been achieved.

Even more valuable is identifying important life goals which may or may not include trading. An exercise which will allow you to do so is the following:

GOAL-SETTING EXERCISE

(i) Identify your goals

▸ Imagine you have just had your 95th birthday and tomorrow your life is to end.

▸ Look back on your life and identify the things you wish you had done.

Fortunately you do not die. Instead, you have been given another chance to do those things you would have liked to have done in your life, but didn't actually do. If these goals are really important to you, you will need to be precise about how you are going to attain them. The second part of the exercise indicates how this might be done.

GOAL-SETTING EXERCISE

(ii) Precise statement of goals

▸ WHY – do I want to do this?

▸ WHEN – am I going to start and when am I going to complete this?

▸ HOW – am I going to do this? What specific, measurable, achievable actions will I take?

▸ WHAT – will I do to prevent this 'I wish I had' from occurring in my life?

I challenge you to take some time now to think about a goal you'd like to pursue. Follow the Goal-Setting Exercise steps and answer each question.

6. NEVER SEEING YOURSELF AS A LOSER, EVEN WHEN YOU LOSE

The sixth and final aspect of superior performance involves never seeing yourself as a loser even when you lose. You are what you label yourself as being.

If you think of yourself as a 'loser', you are a loser.

It's like using the word 'can't'. This puts you in prison.

Terry, a weight lifter I worked with, felt it was impossible for him to lift more than a certain weight. 'I can't lift more than this,' he said. However, once he changed his 'can't' to 'won't', and 'I haven't found a way yet', Terry left the door open for future improvement. He gave himself permission to lift weights heavier than those he had been lifting. Within a couple of days of changing the way he talked to himself, Terry began to improve his lifting performance, shaking himself free of the stagnation that had shackled him for many months.

This is the same pattern as that adopted by the trader referred to earlier who placed a ceiling on his earning potential believing he could not go beyond that. Such a belief often stems from a sense of personal unworthiness, a feeling that 'I do not deserve to make so much money'.

Reframing, or adopting a different viewpoint, is the key to change. If, by looking at something in a particular way, you are unable to improve – 'I can't earn more than X dollars' – then change your viewpoint to 'I haven't yet found a way of earning more than X dollars'. This is your greatest freedom, that of being able to choose the attitude you adopt.

Probably the most powerful reframe you will ever use is this: 'There is no such thing as failure, only information.' Not 'I started making losing trades once I had more than X dollars again. I'll never be able to make more than that', but 'What can I learn from this experience? How can I use the information I get from analysing what happened with those losing trades to improve my performance next time?'

LOUISE'S THOUGHTS

People's love affair with money has always fascinated me. Want to see normal people do completely bizarre things? Add some money and watch the games begin.

How about the friend that disappears after you loan them some money? What's going on there? Or the siblings that create merry hell at the reading of their father's will. Or the bloke with the secret bank account that he isn't telling his wife about. And then there's the girl who spends too much to impress people she doesn't like, with money she doesn't have.

See … it makes ordinary people just crack up!

So is money bad? Of course not. Then what the heck is happening?

Money, in and of itself, is meaningless … until we empower it. We give it meaning, and it's our own thoughts and emotions around money that determine whether it's a positive or negative force in our lives.

I guarantee you this – change your views towards money and what it means to you, and you'll change your results as a trader.

When we realise that money is just a way of keeping score, and it's nothing more than a tool, we detach from its power over us. We stop its control over our thoughts and our actions. Plus, ironically, this attitude paves the way for more of it to enter our lives.

Some of the most greedy, money-hungry people I have ever met have barely any of the stuff. Yet some of the most generous, philanthropic people (who don't continually talk about a lack of money) are some of the most financially wealthy people on the planet.

So which comes first? The attitude about money, or the money itself?

Having trained hundreds of successful traders, and seen them at every stage of their wealth development, I can definitely answer this one. The attitude towards money comes first. The way a trader thinks always precedes their actual share trading results.

In reality, some rich people are poor and some poor people are rich. It's just a matter of time until reality catches up with their mindset.

When does money go from being a positive to a negative force in our lives?

1   When it becomes an obsession, and it's one of the last things you think about before going to sleep, and the first thing you think of when you wake up.

2   If you judge the integrity and calibre of the people you meet by their bank account, their clothes, or the car they drive.

3   If you judge your self-worth by your bank account, your clothes, or the car you drive.

4 If your sense of self is seriously compromised when you either make a lot more money or lose a lot of money.

5 If you are more concerned with money than you are with your health, your relationships, your engagement in new projects, or your enjoyment of a nice night out.

6 When it negatively impacts your most meaningful relationships.

7 When money becomes more important than principles.

I'm not for one minute suggesting that there is any problem with being seriously financially wealthy, if that's your goal. However, I am saying that our views about money can sometimes get out of kilter and damage our emotional wellbeing and our relationships.

So ... how do *your* views about money affect *you*?

To explore this topic further, you're going to want to get the *When Good Trades Attack* pack that I created with Dr Harry Stanton. It's available from www.tradinggame.com.au, and I know you're going to get immediate benefit from it.

Harry is about to tell you about the psychology of change. I know you're not going to want to miss that.

Keep reading to hear what he has to say ...

CHAPTER 7

THE PSYCHOLOGY OF CHANGE

'Out of clutter, find Simplicity. From discord, find Harmony.
In the middle of difficulty lies Opportunity.'

– Albert Einstein

THE ROBBINS APPROACH

Though it has been accepted for many years that psychological change is a long-term process, recent research has indicated that this is not so. It is possible to effect change very quickly, and one approach to doing so has been suggested by Anthony Robbins in his excellent book *Awaken the Giant Within*.

Robbins's initial step involves deciding, quite specifically, what it is that people really want and identifying that which is preventing them from achieving this end. Once this goal is specified, step two involves mobilising the leverage necessary to move people towards its achievement.

To Robbins, this means associating massive pain to not changing now and massive pleasure to the experience of changing now. Such associations create a sense of urgency which overrides people's propensity to perceive change as a 'should' rather than a 'must'.

Believing that knowing why change is necessary is much more important than knowing how it is to be accomplished, Robbins places great emphasis upon assembling very strong reasons for why change should take place. As a means to this end, he uses both pain-inducing questions, such as 'What will this cost me if I do not change?', and pleasure-inducing questions, such as 'What kind of momentum could I create if I make this change in my life?'

Interruption of the limiting pattern is step three. As Robbins points out, in order to get new results in our lives, knowing what we want and getting leverage on ourselves is not enough. By continuing to do the same things and to run the same inappropriate patterns, we are not going to change no matter how highly motivated we may be. However, if we interrupt our limiting patterns of behaviour or emotion by scrambling the sensations we link to our memories, we are more likely to be successful in this endeavour. The main reason why this should be so is that we tend to upset ourselves by the way in which we represent things in our minds. We run the same record over and over again. Instead of continuing to do this, Robbins suggests we take this mental record and scratch it so many times that we cannot experience those feelings anymore. That is what interruption is designed to achieve.

Once the original maladaptive behaviour or emotional pattern has been disturbed in this way, it is necessary to install a new, empowering alternative. This is step four in the model, and it is based on the assumption that the major reason most people's attempts to change are only temporary lies in their failure to find an alternative way of getting out of pain and into the feelings of pleasure.

Step five involves conditioning the new pattern by continual rehearsal, preferably with emotional intensity. Claiming that the brain cannot tell the difference between something vividly imagined and something actually experienced, Robbins suggests that imaginative rehearsal is likely to be equally as effective as actual rehearsal in this conditioning process.

The final step is that of testing through future pacing. People are to imagine the situation or situations which were, in the past, sources of frustration and to notice whether their new pattern has replaced the old. The procedure can be illustrated as shown opposite.

Though all six steps are important, I would like to focus primarily upon the key elements of disrupting the existing maladaptive pattern and replacing it with a more adaptive alternative.

The psychology of change

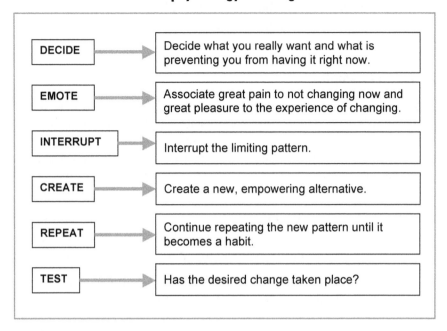

DECIDE →	Decide what you really want and what is preventing you from having it right now.
EMOTE →	Associate great pain to not changing now and great pleasure to the experience of changing.
INTERRUPT →	Interrupt the limiting pattern.
CREATE →	Create a new, empowering alternative.
REPEAT →	Continue repeating the new pattern until it becomes a habit.
TEST →	Has the desired change taken place?

An interruption pattern – the theatre technique

A pattern ideally designed for the interruption of unwanted behaviour is one that combines dissociation, mental imagery, and humour in a very effective 'scratching of the record', which is needed to disrupt old patterns.

1   Imagine you are sitting in the middle of a movie theatre. On the screen before you is a black-and-white snapshot of yourself in a situation just before you had the particular unwanted response.

2   Float out of your body up to the projection booth of the theatre, where you can 'watch yourself watching yourself'. From that position you are able to see yourself sitting in the middle of the theatre, and also see yourself in the still picture which is on the screen.

3   Transform the snapshot up on the screen into a black-and-white movie, which you view from the beginning until just beyond the end of the unwanted experience.

4   When you reach this end point, stop the movie, make it into a slide, turn it into colour, then jump inside the picture and run the movie backwards, taking only one to two seconds to do so.

Everything is to take place in reverse with people walking and talking backwards. As the intent is to make this as amusing as possible, it could be turned into a cartoon and a ridiculous soundtrack added.

A trading example

Let's consider how a maladaptive trading behaviour could be interrupted in this way. James trades commodities and currencies with some success but is unable to trade a stock index. Early in his trading career most of his profits came from trading in this area, but one disastrous trade shattered his confidence to such an extent that the fear of a repeat now prevents him from even looking at this type of contract.

In itself, this is really not a problem because specialisation can be a very profitable way to trade. However, James's behaviour is illustrative in that it is the fear, amounting virtually to a phobia, that needs attention.

This phobia is placing limits upon his behaviour, removing one area of choice from his trading, for it is not that he chooses not to trade a stock index but that he is unable to do so. He fears the stock index to such an extent that he has no freedom as far as it is concerned, no control over his behaviour. It is in such a situation where the cause of the fear is clearly identifiable that the theatre technique works so well.

Although James would usually become quite upset when thinking about the bad stock index trade, using the double dissociation of visualising himself in the audience and in the projection box enabled him to view the experience in a rather detached way, weakening the extremely unpleasant feelings it had previously evoked. This sense of remoteness helped him modify the fear that he had been associating with the situation. Visualising the initially frightening incident in the somewhat ludicrous 'running backwards' mode seemed to achieve an alteration of James's mental perspective, a draining away of negative emotion.

Apparently the human brain learns fear instantly from incidents such as James's losing trade. This fear is initially protective in that it keeps people away from the situations in which they had been damaged. Unfortunately, it can then become overly restrictive, drastically interfering with people's lives. In James's case, he became so frightened of trading a stock index that he would not even look at a chart of these contracts.

However, if the brain can be shown that the incident need no longer be feared, that it could be seen as funny, it can often relinquish the fear. So James imagined himself entering the theatre, sitting down, and seeing himself on the screen just before he was involved in the episode that had proved so traumatic for him. At this point he was looking at himself studying his charts, feeling quite pleased with the improvements he had been making in his technical analysis. After mentally floating up to the projection box, he was then able to look down and simultaneously see himself and this black-and-white slide on the screen.

James then ran the black-and-white movie of the shock involved in learning that his trade had gone against him very badly, stopping it as a slide at the point when he felt reasonably comfortable once again. This was several hours after he had exited the trade and accepted that he had lost badly. Mentally he then entered the picture of himself on the screen, turned it into colour, and ran it backwards as a movie, stopping at the starting point. Instead of picking up the phone to talk to his broker, he was putting it down, his speech was meaningless babble, the lines he had been drawing on his charts jumped back off the page and every action took on a quite ridiculous aspect.

Then he ran the movie forward again in colour, this time remaking it as he would have wished it to happen. In this version the trade was very successful, he made a considerable profit and he felt a sense of confidence in his ability. So in this version of the theatre technique, not only is the unwanted behaviour interrupted but new, desired behaviour is also created.

Another way of accomplishing this is with the 5/1–1/5 technique as described below.

INSTALLING NEW BEHAVIOUR – SUCCESS IMAGERY

Once an existing behaviour/feeling pattern is disrupted, opportunity exists for the installation of the desired new behaviour/feeling. To help yourself install a new behaviour pattern, the following steps can be very helpful. These steps are:

1 inducing a receptive mindset;

2 placing a single suggestion, or a single theme involving a network of suggestions, in the mind; then

3 returning to alertness.

The procedure begins with the use of six deep breaths. The focus is upon the out-breath. As you exhale, count 'five', letting go with the breath. Count 'four' with the next breath, letting go a little more, and continuing to do so with the next three breaths, counting 'three', 'two', and 'one'. On the final breath, as you let go as much as possible, use a key word or words such as 'relax', 'calm', or 'peace'. Then move on to the second step, that of the success scenario.

Should the problem, for example, be that of fear of public speaking, you would 'see' yourself speaking fluently, persuasively, and powerfully to a huge audience, imagining the rapt faces of the audience, your own sense of zest, and the congratulations afterwards.

A very attractive success scenario is thus created in your mind so that, every time you think about it, you prepare your mind to repeat the performance on any future public speaking occasion. When you do come to the actual performance, as far as your mind is concerned, you have already handled it successfully, mentally, many times. Thus, whenever the thought of an impending address crosses your mind, you switch immediately into imagining the success experience. This replaces the fear and anxiety with which you have previously contemplated such a situation.

The final step repeats the six deep breaths pattern, this time emphasis falling upon the in-breath. As you breathe in, count 'one', and imagine you are drawing in alertness and energy. This process continues to the count 'two', 'three', 'four', and 'five', with the next four in-breaths. On the final breath, as you breathe in, use a key word such as 'wide awake', 'energy', 'zest', or 'go' to restore yourself to a state of alertness.

This method not only embodies Robbins's fourth step of new behaviour installation, it also provides the means for achieving his final two steps. Because you are 'seeing' yourself as successful in the future, you are testing the new pattern in the manner Robbins would suggest.

Consider again James's problem of inability to trade a stock index and how the success imagery approach might be of value to him. He could imagine himself sometime in the future receiving his broker's statement in the mail, opening the letter, looking at the information regarding the closing out of a stock index trade, feeling good about the profit that had been made, and enjoying a sense of confidence in his ability to make a successful stock index trade. He might also imagine himself talking with friends over a drink, discussing the present state of the stock market index, and feeling a sense of satisfaction that he had made a trade based on careful analysis which had proven to be very profitable.

With this enjoyable success scenario being implanted in James's mind, every time he thinks about it, he prepares his mind for future success. When he does come to study the stock index charts, as far as his mind is concerned, he has already made, mentally, many successful trades in this market. Thus, whenever the thought of the index crosses his mind, he switches immediately into imagining the success experience. This replaces the fear and anxiety with which he has previously contemplated such a situation.

PROGRAMMING OF THE UNCONSCIOUS

What James was doing was to exert considerable influence over his unconscious mind. As has been emphasised throughout this book, one of the greatest powers you possess lies in your ability to imagine yourself behaving as you want to behave. This success visualisation forms one element in a five-step method which will enable you to take more control over your mind and your trading than you would have ever believed possible.

The first step involves **physical relaxation**, which is induced through concentration upon the breath, following it as it flows in and out, letting go tension, tightness, and discomfort with each out-breath. Such concentration can often create a state of detachment in which people virtually watch themselves breathing.

Mental calmness is the second step, this being encouraged through imagining the mind as a pond, the surface of which is completely still, like a mirror. Thoughts are watched in a detached way, being allowed to drift into one side of the mind, float through above the still water, then disappear out of the other side of the mind. Attention is then returned to further contemplation of the water's stillness.

The next step is the **disposal of 'rubbish'**. People are to imagine themselves 'dumping' mental obstacles such as fears, doubts, worries, and guilt down a chute from which nothing can return. Physical obstacles such as cigarettes and excess weight may also be disposed of in this way.

In the CD I made with Louise called *Relaxation for Traders*, I take you through a guided imagery to help you do this, while listening to my voice. That CD is available from www.tradinggame.com.au.

Removal of a barrier representing everything that is negative in people's lives follows. Embodied in this barrier are self-destructive thoughts, forces of failure and defeat, mental obstacles, and self-imposed limitations; everything that is preventing individuals from enjoying their lives as they would like. This barrier is destroyed through use of the imagination.

Enjoyment of **a special place** where people feel content, tranquil, and still is the last step. In this place they 'turn off' the outside world. Once individuals find their special place, it is suggested that they think of themselves as they want to be, imagining themselves behaving the way they want to behave and 'seeing' themselves achieving the success they wish to achieve.

Opportunities to tailor the approach to handle specific problems associated with trading occur within each of these five steps. Breathing is used as the introduction in this five-step approach but it can be quite helpful to traders in their own right as it permits them to 'let go' of tension, strain, and pressure. When you are too tense, you can use concentration on the breath to replace the tension-creating thoughts which are generating anxiety.

MENTAL CONDITIONING WITH THE 'POND'

A useful way of using the pond is to imagine the area above the water as the conscious part of the mind and that below as the unconscious part. Into this pond of your mind, you can place anything you desire. One way of doing so is through the use of a metaphor, such as the following:

> Imagine that, in your hand, you hold a beautiful stone … the stone of intense concentration … drop this stone into the pond of your mind watching it as it sinks … down … and down … deeper … and deeper … until it comes to rest at the bottom of the pond … the sand covers it and your mind just locks around the idea of intense concentration, radiating it through your entire being … through your mind … it's a feeling you take away with you … one that becomes a permanent part of your life … growing more powerful day by day … you will find you can devote your complete, undivided attention to the event in which you are occupied … nothing will be able to disturb that concentration … it will be as if you were performing within a glass shell which blocks out all distracting influences … they just won't be important … nothing exists but [the chart].

Naturally, you can follow the same procedure with other stones, each one representing a particular attribute relevant to your trading or your life more generally. Mental calmness, physical relaxation, determination, and confidence are all attributes that might be appropriate.

METAPHORS CAN BE VARIED AT WILL

As the needs of traders will vary, the pond, rubbish chute, and barrier metaphors may be adapted to meet individual needs. While some might want to discard cigarettes or alcohol down the chute, others may use it as a means of getting rid of excess weight.

Of particular value to a trader is the opportunity provided to relive a disastrous performance, to remove it from his or her mind, wrap it in a garbage bag, and 'dump' it down the chute, perhaps even throwing a match down the chute in order to ignite the bag and make doubly sure it will not return. Another might want to dispose of illness down the chute, stripping it away from the body and discarding it.

This mental conditioning often accelerates healing, a process which can also be helped by dropping the stone of 'healing' into the pond, suggesting it will work deep within the unconscious mind to assist other treatment the person might be having. Anything that promotes a positive frame of mind toward health is likely to be beneficial.

THE 'SPECIAL PLACE'

This visualisation may also take on many variations. One I have found to be particularly useful is to imagine yourself passing through a door and shutting it behind you to exclude the rest of the world. In this place you imagine you are able to contact the unconscious part of your mind which will then solve any problems you might have. One aspect of such solutions will be that things which have worried or upset you in the past will simply drop out of your life as if they never existed. Because these things have now become so unimportant, you will probably forget you were ever disturbed in this way.

You may want to choose your own special place or simply allow a suitable place to come to you spontaneously as you pass through the door. This could be somewhere enjoyable from your childhood, a fantasy place, a beach, garden, lovely room, or a comfortable bed. Wherever it may be, when you enter it you will feel happy, content, tranquil, and still.

You may wish to close your eyes and withdraw for a moment from the tension of the marketplace. For this to be effective, you must not just 'leave' the market but actually 'arrive' somewhere else – the special place where you are happy, content, and peaceful. Practice will enable you to 'switch off' the world virtually instantly.

Make your 'special place' as real as possible. Imagine the things you would see in this place, their colour, shape, and size; the things you would hear, their volume and tone; the things you would feel, their texture and temperature; the things you would smell; and the things you would taste. You may not be successful in imaginatively recreating all five senses. Perhaps you will be able to make use of only one sense, but use it to create a place for yourself where you feel really good.

When you feel you are in such a place, use a cue to make it easier for you to return. For example, place together the thumb and first finger of your dominant hand, linking this action with the experience of being in your special place, relaxed and comfortable. Now let yourself drift back to your real situation, perhaps sitting in a chair in your home. Test your cue by placing the thumb and finger together, letting yourself return to your special place. Keep this hand position while you relax, then, when you are ready to return to the 'real' world, release the contact of finger and thumb. This cue, once you have practised it a few times, will ease your entry into that restful situation for just the moment that you need it during a break in your activities. It can be especially useful in a tense situation, where your anxiety or arousal level has gone far too high.

TATE ON TRADING

Within the Mentor Program we have been having a bit of a discussion regarding the desperate need for activity that drives many traders.

You see, traditionally Westerners equate activity with productive effort; as such, the more noise and the more fuss you make the more productive you are. The same philosophy drifts into trading. Trading becomes an activity-based endeavour, which then migrates into entertainment.

Research by W.B. Canoles, S.R. Thompson, S.H. Irwin, and V.G. France in their paper *An Analysis of the Profiles and Motivations of Habitual Commodity Speculators* found most tellingly that *being in the action is more important than the financial consequences* for the vast majority of traders they interviewed.

Activity rather than the consequences of that activity are more important to the trader. In the words of Thoreau it appears that *all men lead lives of quiet desperation* and trading is a way of outrunning this desperation. When we consider the reasons behind the motivations of many traders it is easy to see how seductive 'action' related metaphors are to us.

My view of trading is very different. I view trading as a profession of stillness and patience, not activity. This notion can best be described by a series of Japanese philosophical concepts. The first is known as Mushin or no mindedness. Such a notion is often confusing since the idea of no mindedness implies a vacuum with limited resources. This is incorrect; the closest Western concept is unconscious competence – it is a mind that is free from extraneous considerations. As such it is free to act unencumbered by emotion. Mushin by definition is also firmly rooted in the present so notions of past and present are irrelevant, and by extension fear and worry are not present as these concepts depend either upon a concern about events past or a fear of future conse- ◁ quences. Therefore what has occurred with past trades is irrelevant, as is what might happen with any future trades.

The second stage is Zanshin, which is a state of mind that enables you to retain control of both your conscious and unconscious mind while engaged in a course of action. It is the ability to engage both the market and be aware of the impact of your engagement upon your subconscious mind. Zanshin is activity based; you are aware of the trade and all the possible consequences of that trade. Yet the notion of Mushin still permeates this transition since both states of mind are fully present in the moment. Worry cannot seep into the trading system if it is set in the present.

The final phase is Jikishin or the taking of opportunity without fear or hesitation. Consider these moments within the context of a given trade. Trading systems consist of a generic set of principles – a setup followed by a trigger leading to an eventual exit. Mushin is our setup phase; it is our point of stillness where we wait. Zanshin is the movement out of Mushin into an active phase. We have taken our trigger and are aware of all the things that could happen. The notion of Jikishin floats between entry and exit since both require action without fear.

It is easy to see how such a philosophy contradicts that put forward by Western ideals such as the need for a work ethic which in turn prompts traders to create activity for the sake of it. The basic philosophies are very different since one is activity based and the other is based in stillness followed by brief moments of action. Yet at all times your mind remains still and free.

Trading is an internal endeavour since our trading only takes place in our mind. For example, as I write this I have a dealing screen open that is telling me the prices of options on the Dow. My only representation of the market is my screen; my only perception is what my subconscious mind filters. It would be difficult for me to point to the market where these options were traded since that is most likely another aggregation of screens which are in turn reflections of other people's perceptions.

As Harry has pointed out, too often traders look outward for what is essentially an internal problem. The ability to create a calm, still mind solves myriad trading problems, as does the creation of safe metaphors. While notions such as Mushin are difficult for those who are first exposed to them, it is possible to build metaphors that are calm. Other traders have told me that they regard trading as surfing, sailing, or skiing, all endeavours they find pleasant, safe, and most importantly peaceful.

The trading metaphor you choose will have a huge effect on your trading results.

Harry's about to tell you about how to get into the right frame of mind to trade effectively.

Keep on reading to hear his thoughts ...

CHAPTER 8

THE CREATION OF A DESIRED STATE

'If we did all the things we are capable of,
we would astound ourselves.'

– Thomas Edison

ATTITUDE MAKES A DIFFERENCE

Anthony Robbins's framework is a powerful technique which can create effective change. Realising the great importance of attitude is another.

Attitudes

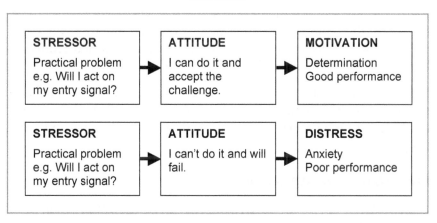

STRESSOR	ATTITUDE	MOTIVATION
Practical problem e.g. Will I act on my entry signal?	I can do it and accept the challenge.	Determination Good performance

STRESSOR	ATTITUDE	DISTRESS
Practical problem e.g. Will I act on my entry signal?	I can't do it and will fail.	Anxiety Poor performance

We have the power to change our attitude about anything and, in a moment, change our states and behaviour. Many people who have experienced great traumas look back on these as the most valuable experiences of their lives. This time provided an opportunity for them to grow in new directions – a growth that would not have taken place had their normal routine existence continued uninterrupted by the trauma. As has been often said, as one door closes, another opens.

John's panic attacks

John, a trader of my acquaintance, was experiencing severe panic attacks. This panic apparently stemmed from feelings of discomfort he would feel in his chest. The meaning he attached to these feelings was: 'There is something wrong with my heart. I'm going to have a heart attack and die.'

Although he had his heart examined by several specialists, he still believed there was something faulty with his heart. At the recurrence of the discomfort, he would enter the panic state with extreme sweating, dizziness, elevated pulse rate, and trembling hands.

Now John had just learned to windsurf, an activity he really loved. Fortunately we are able to imagine ourselves doing things in such a way that we recapture part or all of the original enjoyment. So John, at the slightest sign of the chest discomfort, went windsurfing in his imagination. What he did was attach a different meaning to the discomfort. Instead of it being, 'I'm going to have a heart attack and die', it became, 'Let's go windsurfing'. In the three years since he has made this change, John has not had a panic attack, though he still experiences the chest pain which doctors have been unable to diagnose.

John's success has occurred because he has separated what actually exists (the discomfort) from what he had been adding to it (the panic attacks). He has distanced himself from this behaviour and redirected himself towards something that was very positive, the windsurfing.

By acting in this way he changed the state he was in. This is, I believe, the greatest power we have and one that we consistently underestimate, allowing our mood states to be controlled by external events and other people.

Creating the state we desire

Some of the ways in which we can take more control over our own states of mind are listed here:

CREATING THE STATE WE DESIRE

To create the state we desire we need to control
our physiology and our mental focus.

▸ PHYSIOLOGY – smile, laugh, skip, slap body, pump fist

▸ MENTAL FOCUS

    – Words – Create your own meaning: reframe.

    – Questions – 'For what am I grateful this day?'

    – Metaphors – 'Life is a dance.'

    – Beliefs and rules – 'What has to happen for me to feel good?'

Physiology – in this context – means using your body the way you would use it when you were in the state you wanted to be in.

If you want to be miserable, for example, walk slowly, dragging yourself along, hang your head, look down and frown. This will make sure you feel bad.

However, if you wake up feeling like this and want to change your mood state then walk as if you were happy, energetically, with bounce in your step, smile, laugh, put your shoulders back and look up. Slap your body and punch the air.

It takes considerable effort to make yourself do this when you feel low but, after a few minutes, you really start feeling better. Many psychologists have pointed out that if we want to feel a particular way we must act as if we are already in that state. To feel happy, energetic, and confident we must act as if we are already that way.

Using physiology in the way I have suggested is a very powerful way of creating the state we desire.

Mental focus is linked to changing physiology. It is not much good to assume, physically, the behaviour of a happy person if your thoughts are gloomy and negative. To feel positive and on top of things you have to concentrate your mind on positive thoughts, beliefs, metaphors, words, and questions, for these are all ways of achieving the focus you desire. For example, the actual words you use can exert a tremendous influence upon your mental state, particularly as to whether you feel stressed or not.

Don't exaggerate the significance of problems

▸ We produce irrational beliefs by using inappropriate words such as 'unbearable' to describe minor events like being held up in traffic.

▸ More appropriate words are 'inconvenient', 'unfortunate', 'annoying'.

Avoid words indicating demands

▸ We create negative responses in ourselves and others by using 'must', 'should', 'ought to'.

▸ Instead use 'I would rather…', 'I would prefer…'

Avoid the labels 'good' and 'bad'

▸ Labelling implies unrealistic absolutes – rarely is anything black or white.

▸ When we judge, criticise, or moralise, we create negative emotions within ourselves.

▸ If you cannot change things or people, then accept them as they are.

What questions do you ask yourself?

So it is important to talk to yourself in ways that strengthen you, not weaken you. The same is true for the questions you ask yourself.

Because our life experience is based on whatever we focus on, questions such as the following direct our minds into positive directions so that you are likely to experience more happiness, excitement, pride, gratitude, joy, commitment, and love every day of your life. As Robbins – to whom I referred earlier – puts it, quality questions create a quality life. See if you can arrive at two or three answers to all of these questions. If you have difficulty discovering an answer simply add the word 'could'. For example, 'What could I be most happy about in my life now?'

METAPHORS

As Chris Tate mentioned at the end of the previous chapter, the metaphors you use to describe your life are very influential. There is a vast gulf between the attitude indicated by 'Life wasn't meant to be easy' and that suggested by 'Life is a dance'. One metaphor I have found particularly valuable in assisting the clients with whom I work is that of 'The Lake'.

The Lake

'See' yourself standing on the shore of a lake, looking out over the water. Where you stand, it is a dreary and depressing scene, the water rough and treacherous, whipped into waves by wind and rain. Yet, the other side of the lake is quite different, with people enjoying the bright sunshine and lively atmosphere. This is the shore of health and normality.

Visualise yourself crossing the lake in some way that requires considerable effort. Rowing a boat, paddling a canoe, or even swimming would be possibilities. Not only are the waves and wind to be combated, other obstacles will impede your progress from the shore of dreariness to the shore of brightness, but these you overcome. If the distance seems too great, or your efforts are exhausting you, use the islands dotting the surface of the lake as temporary resting places.

When you finally reach the bright shore, as you will, you feel a tremendous surge of confidence, a belief in your ability to live your life as you want to, coping effectively and happily with whatever your environment provides. As you look back towards the shore you have just left, it is no longer visible. A mist has arisen, blotting it from view and from your life.

The Lake exercise allows you to leave behind metaphors that have been impeding you, such as 'The market is out to get me', 'I'm so unlucky, always getting in and out of the market at the wrong times', and 'Nothing ever works right for me'. These stay on the dreary shore, blotted out of your life, and are replaced by the positive metaphors of the bright shore such as 'I am a winner' and 'Day by day in every way I am becoming a better trader'.

BELIEFS AND RULES

The beliefs and rules by which you live also influence your attitude and your state of mind very powerfully.

You may enjoy dancing, but you will only go dancing if no-one is smoking in the room, or if the music is not too loud, or if there is no crowding on the dance floor. With rules like these you are not going to go dancing very often. Or you may believe that you can only truly love someone if they are tall, handsome or beautiful, blonde, blue-eyed, considerate, with a wonderful sense of humour, and wealthy. The list may be endless. Again, there are unlikely to be too many people who measure up as worthy of your love.

There are many ways of feeling good and there may be even more ways of feeling bad, according to the beliefs and rules you live by. Unfortunately, it has been my experience that people are generally better at the latter than at the former.

15-Minute Change Technique

When I am working with clients well launched into their tale of woe, going back over the past and dredging up everything that has been and is wrong in their lives, I will sometimes interrupt them, asking them to tell me something really good that happened in their lives. I ask them something they feel wonderful about.

Simply doing this will change their state, but I will then use a technique I call the 15-Minute Change Technique to enhance the great power of that positive memory so that it completely overshadows the negative material.

This technique is not only very quick, it is also easy to learn, and my clients can then use it to alleviate a wide range of problems, including those affecting their trading.

The ingredients of this piece of magic, drawn primarily from Richard Bandler's book *Time for a Change*, are as follows:

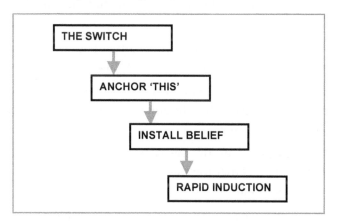

Step 1: The switch

The first step of the 15-Minute Change Technique is 'the switch'. You begin with a picture in your mind of an unwanted behaviour which is made large, colourful, and bright. You might, for instance, 'see' yourself reading a report in the financial press and panicking because it suggests your current position is wrong.

A more desirable behaviour is pictured in black and white, occupying the bottom right-hand corner of this first picture. You might, for example, see yourself reading the same item, smiling gently to yourself as you accept the likelihood that your position is a good one because it is not supported by the 'news'.

As quickly as possible, switch the two pictures, changing their size and colour. After this switch, the two pictures are reset to their original format. Continue this process until you are unable to reset the pictures.

The small black and white picture of the unwanted behaviour is then moved up high to your left, down to the lower left, placed on edge, and spun like a top. As it spins it is made grey and dim, shrinking down to postage-stamp size. It is then moved up to your right, placed a few centimetres in front of your face, shifted to a similar distance over your head, and again shifted to the same distance behind your head.

As it is moved further and further behind you, it finally reaches a point where it disappears. The wanted picture is made small and gradually expanded until it becomes life size. At the same time, the colour and brightness is turned up to reflect the very bright future that lies ahead.

Step 2: Anchoring with 'this'

The second step of the 15-Minute Change Technique is anchoring with 'this'.

The technique follows the switch procedure. The 'wonderful feeling' memory will be the positive picture used at that time.

With closed eyes, take the picture associated with this experience and make 'this' bigger; make 'this' brighter; make 'this' more colourful; intensify 'this' in every way.

The feeling is anchored by the verbal anchor of 'this'. A kinaesthetic anchor, say placing together the thumb and first two fingers of the non-dominant hand, could also be used.

Then think of some negative situations where you behave in ways about which you feel uneasy and, with each situation, close your eyes on whatever it is. As you do, feel 'this' and trigger your kinaesthetic anchor.

It is quite likely that you will no longer find these situations so negative. They could even become enjoyable.

Step 3: Install belief

The third step of the 15-Minute Change Technique is to 'install belief'.

Think of something in which you absolutely believe. 'Tomorrow the sun will rise' could be such a belief.

Now think of a belief that could or could not be true; for example, there is doubt about whether you could dismiss the 'expert' opinion in the financial news without experiencing some level of discomfort.

The two beliefs, one certain and one doubtful, are considered one at a time and the differences between them observed.

In particular, the position in the mind where each of the two beliefs is located is ascertained. Is one directly in front and the other up to the left? Is one up high and the other lower down?

Their brightness, distance, clarity, colour, size, shape, and movement are identified and the differences between them noted. If voices, sounds, or feelings are involved, these differences are observed also until both the unquestioned belief and the doubtful belief are clearly distinguished from each other. The doubtful belief is slowly moved away into the horizon until it hits a point. Then it is pulled back very quickly into the position where the strong and powerful belief is located and the doubtful belief is made identical to the strong and powerful belief in terms of size, colour, brightness, and closeness. This must be done very suddenly so it seems to slot into place with a physical impact.

Step 4: Trance induction

The fourth and final step of the 15-Minute Change Technique is 'trance induction'.

Extend your arm out in front of you with your thumb sticking up into the air. Focus all your attention on your thumbnail. Observe how your eyes change focus, blinking more frequently, as your arm and thumb-nail is gradually brought closer to you. At some spot before your hand reaches your face, you will find your eyes wanting to close. Let them do this, take a deep breath, relax, going all the way down into a trance. Your hand is to remain where it stopped, in a lifted position.

This hand and arm then sinks down only at the speed that you are ready to learn something of great importance.

You recall your very good feeling from 'the switch'. With each breath you go deeper and deeper, enjoying the process of knowing you can learn from your unconscious mind whatever is necessary to solve your particular problem.

Your unconscious will spread your good feeling through your mind and body as you go into a deep, pleasant trance. When your hand settles on your lap you will have learnt whatever you needed to know to handle the situation that was bothering you.

A bit strange?

This all might seem a little strange to readers unused to using their unconscious minds, or those who regard trance states as odd or unusual.

Actually, it is harder to stay out of a trance state than to go into one. Each day we drift in and out of a trance when, for example, we drive a car and cannot remember the last 10 kilometres, or we become so engrossed in a book that we do not hear the doorbell.

All that I am suggesting is that it can be helpful to take some control over this process so you can use deliberately induced trances to help yourself.

The mind accepts suggestion much more powerfully under such conditions. This enables you to feed in positive material relating to your trading so that you are more likely to behave in ways that produce profits than in ways that produce losses.

CHANGE THROUGH BREATHING

It is also possible to achieve change through various breathing techniques.

Perhaps the most effective of these – a Zen Buddhism method – is one I shall describe as 'Zen breathing'.

While retaining the basic concept of following your breath – that is, simply watching it flow in and out without interruption – you add further elements to this basic pattern.

A case in point is that of Kathy, a novice trader who became highly anxious once she had placed a trade. She went a long way towards solving her problem by learning to calm her mind through a practice of the Zen breathing approach, which involves the following steps:

▶ watching her breath and 'seeing' the number '1' in her mind as it flowed in;

▶ mentally taking the number '1' down to a position just below her navel as the breath flowed out;

- 'seeing' the number '2' with her next intake of breath;

- mentally taking the number '2' down to her body centre just below the navel;

- repeating this process with each breathing cycle until the number '10' had been placed in the body centre; then

- beginning another set of 10.

Kathy made no effort to change the flow of her breath, simply counting each one as it flowed in and transferring the focus of her attention from her mind to her body centre. By the time she concluded her first set of 10 breaths she would usually feel relatively calm and relaxed, the anxiety over the trade having virtually disappeared.

This method is astonishingly effective also as a pain killer, even in cases of quite severe pain. In this case it would probably be necessary to do several sets of 10 breaths, but this is certainly a safer, and usually more long-lasting, way of handling pain than the use of drugs.

CREATING A RESOURCE STATE

Yet another way of achieving change is to be able to tap into an optimum internal state of psychological excellence whenever you want to. That is, you are able to call on the highly positive state whenever you need to be at your best. The state is established in the present, but it is based on a past memory.

- Recall a time when you did something extraordinarily well. Ask yourself:

   'What three or four things did I see at that time?' 'What three or four things did I hear?' 'What three or four things did I feel?'

- Use a kinaesthetic anchor such as touching the back of one hand with a finger of the other hand, placing thumb and forefinger together, or clenching your fist when the memory of the experience peaks in intensity. Use a physical action you do not usually make.

- Test this to find whether you can then bring back the feeling of the state of excellence using your own touch. If this doesn't happen, repeat the procedure until your touch does recall the optimum state.

THE CLENCHED FIST TECHNIQUE

Another way of creating a resource state is with the clenched fist technique. This is another way of using a conditioned trigger or anchor to facilitate the changing of troublesome emotional states. When you use it, it arouses a positive mood state within you which is then conditioned to the cue of a clenched fist, ready for use whenever required. In addition, you will be able to let go of negative feelings and replace them with the previously conditioned pleasant emotional state. It is a technique particularly well adapted to the generation of confidence, the way it was used by Michael, a 37-year-old stockbroker who traded commodities.

Michael remembered three occasions on which he had made very profitable trades. As he imagined himself back in the first of these situations, 'seeing' the things he would have seen, 'hearing' the things he would have heard, and 'feeling' the things he would have felt, a very positive image was created. This made Michael feel very good, and as he experienced this feeling, he clenched the fist of his dominant hand, thus creating a mental association. He continued to build up the power of the experience, taking a couple of deep breaths to help the process along.

When the feelings became very strong, he unclenched his hand, but the positive feelings stayed with him. This procedure was repeated for the second and third situations which he had remembered, the link between clenching of the fist and feeling good being strengthened each time so that Michael conditioned himself to re-experience the desired feelings whenever he clenched the fist of his dominant hand.

Once this positive pattern had been conditioned, Michael drifted back into the past to a time when he felt a negative state which he wanted to control, a state involving indecision, self-doubt, and anxiety. When these negative feelings were present, he clenched his non-dominant left hand, thinking of it as an incredibly powerful magnet attracting all the unwanted physical and emotional knots within him. The unpleasant feelings funnelled down through his shoulder and arm into his fist where they were locked up tightly.

Once he had moved all, or most, of the negative feelings in this way, Michael squeezed his dominant right hand into a strong, confident, happy fist, evoking the elation associated with his best trading performances and, as he did so, simultaneously opened his non-dominant hand, allowing the unpleasant feelings to flow away, evaporating into nothingness.

In this way, he replaced his unwanted negative emotional state with a more pleasurable positive one. In particular, confidence replaced self-doubt. Once the transformation had been achieved, Michael opened his right hand and the positive mood state remained with him as it had been conditioned to do.

LOUISE'S THOUGHTS

There are so many things to be fearful of in the markets. Fear of taking a loss, fear of learning a new skill, fear of failure, fear of what others think of your decisions – the list goes on and on. To be successful in the sharemarket you must overcome these fears, and strive to achieve trading excellence. To quote Lao Tzu (born in 604 BC and known as the Father of Taoism), 'Conquering others requires force, conquering oneself requires strength'.

There is one other predominant fear that people struggle with in the markets – the fear of success. Can you visualise how your life would be if your net worth doubled, or tripled? This skill is essential in order to attain your goals. To attain greatness, you have to have the courage to visualise it.

Traders brought up in a religious environment may also struggle with the question of ethics. Is it okay to be rich? Is there a higher level of nobility in suffering and being the revered 'battler' who is almost worshipped within Australian culture?

You will need to come to grips with these issues in order to develop wealth. Money doesn't change people – it only amplifies their natural predisposition. If it is in your nature to be kind and good to your fellow man then money will assist you in this goal. Your contributions to charity can be more significant.

Depending on your upbringing, you may have different views on the value of money and what it can mean to you personally. Often inspired from a religious basis, many traders inadvertently sabotage their own livelihood because of their view that money is evil. This can be on an unconscious level, as even though we are surrounded by materialistic goals, some people allow statements to creep into their conversations that can be detrimental to their financial wellbeing. Have you ever heard that 'money is the root of all evil', or if you see an expensive car driving past have you thought to yourself, 'They must be drug dealers'? If so, your views about money may be seriously affecting your trading results.

One of the simplest ways to stop these types of thoughts from affecting us is to make them explicit. By spelling out exactly what your beliefs are, you may be able to boost your awareness and then eventually diminish their hold over your life. This exercise will help you do just this.

It's your turn ...

Fill in this section without thinking about each statement in great detail. Even if you think some of the areas discussed overlap, complete each statement shown. Just use the first words that come into your head.

People who have money are:

_____

_____

My mother always told me that money:

_____

_____

If I had enough money I would:

_____

_____

Money tells people you:

_____

_____

I use money to:

_____

_____

Money allows you to:

_____

_____

If money was no object I would:

_____

_____

Money is:

_____

_____

Dad thinks money:

_____

_____

The best thing about money is:

_____

_____

The richest person I know made his/her money by:

_____

_____

Money comes to those who:

_____

_____

In my family, people who have money are:

_____

_____

Money can help:

_____

_____

The worst thing about money is:

_____

_____

People with money are:

_____

_____

If someone doesn't have much money they are:

_____

_____

Enough money will let you:

_____

_____

If I had lots of money, people would:

_____

_____

My family thinks money:

_____

_____

Eventually, I hope to have enough money to:

_____

_____

The scariest thing about money is:

_____

_____

Money lets me:

_____

_____

I really want to use my money to:

_____

_____

My main influencer in the field of money is:

_____

_____

When I was a kid there was never enough money to:

_____

_____

Have a look at your list of thoughts about money. Are there any themes present that you feel may help or hinder your progress with trading? Where did your thoughts about money come from? Do you feel that any of these ideas are holding you back as a trader? Take some time to detail your thoughts about money here:

_____

_____

_____

_____

_____

In this chapter we have focused on techniques that allow you to take more control over your mental state. Though all these techniques have worked well for many people on many occasions, not all of them will necessarily help you create your desired state. It is a matter of experimentation, of finding which one or ones best suit your personality and produce the results you want. Practise these, become very good at using them, particularly in the ways outlined in the next chapter, and do not concern yourself with the other techniques that do not seem so productive for you.

Harry's about to tell you how to win at playing the Trading Game. Keep on reading to hear his views...

CHAPTER 9

PLAYING THE TRADING GAME

'Success is not final, failure is not fatal: it is the
courage to continue that counts.'

– Winston Churchill

In an earlier chapter I referred to Gallwey's concept of the Inner Game.
This is played against those internal mental and emotional obstacles
which interfere with our performance by encouraging us to worry,
agonise, and become upset. The importance of this game to the trader
is illustrated in the following comparison of top and average traders.

The inner game of trading

MOST TRADERS:

- Identify market signal.

- Confused, anxious, or
  inconsistent reaction.

- Feel 'bad' (angry,
  nervous, hesitant)
  about the trade.

TOP TRADERS:

- Identify market signal.

- React automatically
  with confidence.

- Feel 'good' (confident,
  high self-esteem) about
  the trade.

INNER OBSTACLES TO SUCCESSFUL TRADING

What is it that causes most traders to behave in this self-defeating manner, one which stops them from playing the trading game more successfully and achieving what they want? One possible answer is the obstacles that exist within their own minds. Four of the most common inner obstacles are as follows:

Common inner obstacles

1. Failure to realise that you can control only yourself, not the markets.

2. Failure to realise that you alone are completely responsible for the outcomes of your actions.
   - ▸ Inflexible perception.
   - ▸ The unstructured nature of the market.

3. Losing the edge.

4. Your beliefs.

YOU CAN ONLY CONTROL YOURSELF – NOT THE MARKETS

Just as you do not have the power to control or manipulate the market yourself, the market has no power or control over you. The responsibility for what you perceive and for your resulting behaviour is totally yours. Because of this, you are free to structure the game inside your mind in any particular way you please because it is you alone who decides whether the game begins or ends.

That means, if you are behaving in a way that is not getting you where you want to go, you will have to change this inner structure.

The more experience you gain as a trader, the more you will realise that trading is primarily a mental activity. It isn't an Outer Game of 'You' versus 'The Markets'. It's an Inner Game of 'You' against 'The Obstacles Thrown Up By Your Own Mind'.

Instead of looking at other traders as competitors against whom you must battle, you might prefer to think of them as giving you the opportunity to profit from their divergent views of future market direction. This is comparable to loving your tennis opponents for the opportunity they give you to draw on your own inner resources and become the player you are capable of becoming. So, too, the markets offer you, the individual trader, the stimulation which can enable you to become as good a trader as you are capable of being.

Once you accept that you alone are completely responsible for your actions, you can assume control over your own trading behaviour. It is not the market that creates the ways in which you see it. Rather, the market serves as a mirror, reflecting what is going on inside of you at any particular time. A rally, for example, has no objective meaning in itself. It is you who provides this meaning, depending on whether you are long or short, missed a profitable trade or stayed out of a losing trade. The way you perceive the market is a creation of your own mind. From the myriad alternatives available, you choose one.

Probably the most fundamental difference that distinguishes winning traders from those who lose is that the former know they are responsible for their results, while the latter think, or at least behave as if, they are not. To win consistently, it is essential you accept complete responsibility for results you produce. So, although you may not be able to control what the markets do, you can control the way you perceive them so that you become far more objective, far more detached. If you cannot accept responsibility for your own actions, you cannot improve your performance. You are destined to repeat the same mistakes, for you have not accepted that they could be your mistakes.

THE IMPORTANCE OF YOUR BELIEFS

To be successful as a trader, you need an edge.

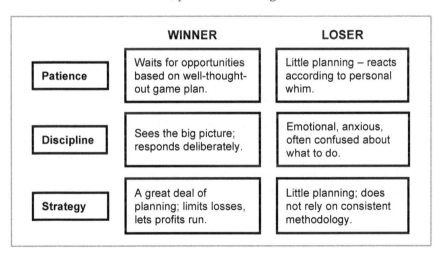

	WINNER	LOSER
Patience	Waits for opportunities based on well-thought-out game plan.	Little planning – reacts according to personal whim.
Discipline	Sees the big picture; responds deliberately.	Emotional, anxious, often confused about what to do.
Strategy	A great deal of planning; limits losses, lets profits run.	Little planning; does not rely on consistent methodology.

To create a winner's edge for yourself is actually a function of your beliefs, for your beliefs tend to affect your behaviour quite strongly.

Unfortunately most people's beliefs are negative rather than positive because they give more weight, in their minds, to what they cannot do rather than what they can do.

The following diagram illustrates two different sets of beliefs about the market – one set is limiting; the other resourceful.

Beliefs about the market

UNIVERSAL BELIEFS	
LIMITING The markets are rigged. The market doesn't let you win.	**RESOURCEFUL** The markets provide an opportunity. The markets exist to give me profits.
BELIEFS ABOUT YOURSELF	
LIMITING I'm an idiot – how could I have made such a stupid trade?	**RESOURCEFUL** Everyone makes mistakes; I'll just focus on the next trade.
RULES TO LIVE BY	
LIMITING If the market doesn't do what I expect it to, then I don't know anything.	**RESOURCEFUL** If the market doesn't do as I expect, then I may need to re-analyse.

The difference between positive and negative ways of thinking emerge very strongly in the above diagram.

Limiting beliefs prevent us doing what we are perfectly capable of achieving, and unless we make a change in this area we will certainly not have any form of winning edge. However, before you can make such a change you require an awareness of your current beliefs.

It is the self-observation concept. Until you know what you are doing now you are unable to do something different to improve matters. By honestly answering the following questions you will be able to identify what it is that you currently believe about the market and your attempts to trade it successfully:

▸ List beliefs you now hold about yourself that detract from your trading.

▸ List beliefs about yourself which, if adopted, would improve your trading.

- List beliefs you now hold about the market that undermine you.

- List five 'if…then' rules that currently control your trading.

Once you have the answers to these questions, see how they compare with the following belief systems which distinguish the market winners from the market losers:

WINNERS BELIEVE	LOSERS BELIEVE
- Money is not that important.	- Money is the most important thing.
- The profits will automatically flow if I follow my trading rules.	- Making money is more important than trading well.
- Losing is part of the process. ◁	- I must not lose any money.
- Trading is a game; it is fun.	- Trading is a serious business.
- I know I can win.	- I have to trade well to pay the rent.
- There is no such thing as failure.	- I know they are going to get me; I'm going to lose again.
- Every setback provides me with new market information ◁ and experience.	- I'm a failure.
- IF I am to be a successful trader, THEN I must be patient.	- IF I'm patient, THEN I will miss the market.
- IF I get stopped out, THEN I have learned something ◁ important.	- IF I get stopped out of the market, THEN I'm unlucky.
- IF I am a disciplined trader, THEN I will consistently apply ◁ my trading rules.	- IF I apply my trading rules, THEN I won't be able to adjust to sudden market moves.
- IF I take a loss, THEN it is a ◁ normal part of the process.	- IF I take a loss, THEN I am a loser.

(handwritten: unacceptable)

(handwritten: — aiming at 60/40 is like hoping to come 3rd in a 2 person race/)

(handwritten notes in right margin: 3rd in a 2 person race / 1st, 2nd / but 1 out / else.)

Most of us spend our lives trying to change what is in front of us, the outer reality, to suit the makeup of our inner environment, our inner reality.

It is far easier and much more effective to change the way we think about what is in front of us. Then we are able to change the quality of our experience of it. That is, by changing our perception, we change our reality. Let's say you decided that 'any single trade is inconsequential because it is only one of the next thousand trades I am going to make'. Acceptance of such a belief could be of great value to you in its power to reduce anxiety and help you trade more calmly. Once you accept such a belief, it exerts control over how you process information in the following way:

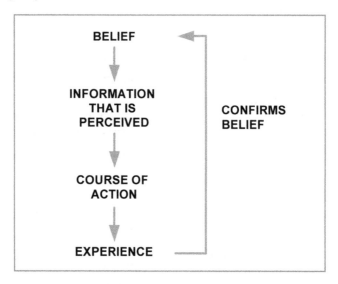

Our beliefs control what we pay attention to

This perception influences how we behave, then, as a result of the course of action we adopt, we experience things in a certain way which, in turn, provides feedback to support us in our belief. It is a closed system.

This is very valuable to us as traders if our beliefs are leading to better trading and thus increased equity. Believing in the essential triviality of any one trade may help us achieve this success by engendering the detachment and emotional discipline that is so necessary. On the other hand, we need to be open to the new information that could lead to new experiences, or else we will continually experience the above closed-loop nature of our beliefs. So install those beliefs that you find helpful to your success as a trader, but practise self-observation to increase your openness to new information leading to other beliefs that might be even more helpful.

SUBMODALITIES

A belief shared by traders who are consistently successful is that the market is always right. In this way they release themselves from the fear of being wrong. They also believe in the value of establishing definite trading rules and sticking to them. Possibly of even more importance is their ability to think in ways that empower them, not weaken them.

This is a question that should concern us all – what thoughts and beliefs are we allowing to control our lives? If they are negative ones which are undermining our effectiveness as traders and as human beings we need to change them, and one interesting way of doing so is the 'submodalities technique'.

Graham's story

Graham, who had worked as an engineer for most of his life, was casting about for something to do in his retirement, which was only about six months in the future. While speaking with a friend who did some part-time trading on the stock market he became infected with his friend's enthusiasm and decided that trading seemed to be just what he was looking for.

He read a number of books on trading and attended several seminars advertised as providing the expertise necessary for trading the market successfully. He also paper traded for some time, telling himself he would commence in earnest once his retirement was finalised.

Once he had retired, Graham established an account with a broker, and set up his study for trading with a computer and the appropriate software for technical analysis. However, when the time came, he found he just could not actually pick up the telephone to enter the trade. Whenever he identified a trade that met the rules he had worked out for himself, he talked himself out of doing anything.

In other words, he lacked confidence in his ability to trade successfully.

He continued to talk with his friend and a couple of other acquaintances who did some trading, he read books, attended seminars, and, through his computer, accessed various financial information newsgroups.

Unfortunately, several of his trading acquaintances had come badly unstuck on a particular trade and the horror stories they told further eroded his confidence. In his mind, he had this thought of financial ruin; of all the money he had accumulated lost to the market. Yet, he felt trading was something he at least wanted to try.

As I worked with Graham, I had him think about the weakening thought of financial ruin and identify a mental picture associated with it. This turned out to be an image of himself living in poverty. He described this picture, visualising it as being close to him, large, bright, sharply focused, and colourful. By seeing it in this way, Graham had made it extremely powerful. He then varied each of these submodalities – that is, distance, brightness, focus, and colour – one at a time, in an effort to discover which one or ones would diminish the power of the picture and of the thought.

First he shrunk the picture. This helped a little. Then he pushed it well away into the distance, experiencing an instantaneous effect of its power being reduced. After bringing it back close, Graham made the outlines fuzzy and unfocused, a change which also helped him feel better. Turning down the brightness achieved nothing, nor did removing all the colour and making it black and white. Placing a frame around the picture also led to a considerable reduction in its power.

The variations that worked best for Graham were shifting the picture out of focus, pushing it well away into the distance, framing it, and hanging it on the wall. By doing this, he reduced the power of the particular thought to upset him. Immediately he replaced it with another thought which brought him pleasure, a time when an engineering project which he had planned had won a national award. The picture accompanying this thought was brought up very close, sharply focused, and had no frame around it.

When I spoke with Graham five months later, he told me that he had been able to initiate trades without any difficulty and was moderately successful in terms of his profits exceeding his losses. In other words, instead of being controlled by the negative thought of failure, he had now assumed more control over his thought process, choosing to think in ways that empowered, rather than weakened, him.

Of course, Graham may not have been able to 'see' a picture in his mind accompanying the worrying thought. Some people are unable to do so, though not as many as is popularly supposed. In this case, he may have heard an internal voice. Should this have been the case, whenever he was contemplating putting on a trade, he would perhaps hear the voice of his father telling him that he had no head for money, or that he always was doing the wrong thing financially, or some other negative message parents give their children. Graham, as a result of having internalised these messages, could easily believe he would never be good at anything that had to do with money. As long as he allows that voice to remain as it is, it will continue to affect his life.

To change the focus of control from the inner voice to himself, Graham would give his father's voice definite characteristics such as volume, speed, accent, and distance. These he varied, one at a time. Pushing the voice well away into the distance seemed to reduce its power somewhat but none of the other submodalities appeared to be particularly effective. The change, according to Graham, that really did make a difference was to make his father sound like Donald Duck gargling underwater. The result was so ridiculous that Graham could no longer take the negative messages seriously and the power of his father's voice to influence his behaviour was removed.

Should Graham neither 'see' pictures or 'hear' voices, he might experience a feeling. Whenever the point came for putting on a trade, Graham might become aware of a feeling of absolute dread. Using the same pattern as that outlined above, I would have Graham describe the feeling. Let's say he located it in his abdomen, experiencing it as black, heavy, cold, circular in shape, and quite large. He would then be able to shift the unpleasant feeling outside his body, change the colour to a pleasant green, warm it in front of the radiator, compress it into a cube, and throw it out the window. It's all about changing something unwanted and negative into something wanted and positive.

By making such a change you reduce the power of the external environment to influence your inner environment. By changing submodalities as I have outlined above, you change the thought and feeling so that it is no longer the same. Once you have done so, it can no longer influence you in the same way.

THE SWISH

This is another way of taking increased control over the way you think. The technique embraces several steps, the first of these being the identification of context. This is to determine where or when people would like to behave or respond differently than they are now doing. If you wished to lose weight, for instance, you might identify the kitchen as the situation where changed behaviour might be helpful. The second step entails identification of a cue picture, clarifying what it is that you actually see in that situation, just before you begin doing the behaviour that you would like to change. You are seeing this through your own eyes, but without seeing yourself in it. This cue picture might be of your hand reaching out for the refrigerator door. Creating an outcome picture comes next, this being how you would see yourself differently if you had already accomplished the desired change. Adjust this image until it is really attractive, creating a strong belief that the desired change is possible. An appropriate outcome picture might be one of yourself standing on a set of scales which were registering the weight you wished to be, or looking at a trading statement showing a large profit derived from a well-executed trade.

You begin the actual 'swish' by seeing the cue picture big and bright, with eyes closed, then mentally placing a small, dark image of the outcome picture in its lower right-hand corner. This small, dark image is to be mentally 'zoomed' so that it grows big and bright, completely covering the first picture, which will become dim and vanish. The process must be fast, taking only one or two seconds. Once the swish has taken place, the mind is blanked out or the eyes opened. This procedure is repeated a total of five times, each time with a blanking out of the screen or an opening of the eyes as the end of each 'swish'.

The final step is a test, with the first image being pictured. If the 'swish' has been effective, this will be difficult to do, for the picture will tend to fade away and be replaced by the second image, that of the person as he or she wants to be. Should this not occur, it is necessary to repeat the swish pattern.

Jane's story

Jane, a 27-year-old primary school teacher, was new to the trading game. Her father and brother both traded shares and her husband was interested in the futures market. However, none of them did particularly well, having occasional winning streaks among longer losing periods. Jane became quite interested in their talk about trading and wanted to learn more about it. She felt her relatives seemed to be going about it the wrong way but she did not have sufficient experience to work out what they were doing wrong. She decided to attend some seminars on the topic and, although deriving some benefit from these, she found they were really not addressing the questions she had in her mind. Unfortunately, Jane, shy and retiring by nature, was unable to ask these questions. On an occasion when, for any reason, she became the centre of attention, her timidity caused her to feel acutely embarrassed. This would be the situation should she ask a question during the seminar.

Using the swish, Jane closed her eyes and saw the picture of herself sitting quietly in the seminar, too embarrassed to ask a question. Down in the right-hand corner of this picture, she placed a tiny picture of herself standing up and asking a question of the seminar leader. Then Jane swished images, as I've explained above. After six repetitions, she tested and found it quite difficult to mentally 'see' the unwanted picture.

This swishing was all that was required for Jane to overcome her fear of speaking in front of people. She was able to ask questions or to give explanations fluently and easily without any signs of nervousness or agitation. This was not only in the seminar situation, which was the primary source of difficulty, but in all other areas of her life where such behaviour was required.

I would also like to report another happy outcome for Jane. Unfortunately, despite the seminars and wide reading into technical trading techniques, she made very little profit from her activities. However, she did have a lot of enjoyment and, at least, usually finished each year on the profit side of the ledger, unlike her family who remained perennial losers. Part of her relative success compared with the other family members was due to the way in which she established goals for herself.

Goal achievement

One of the great benefits of learning the dynamics of goal achievement is the help it provides you in staying positively focused on what you want, rather than on what you don't want. The particular goal-setting process used by Jane was the following:

1. Select **one area of concentration** especially meaningful for you. For example, trading.

2. Within this area, select one **payoff area** where you would most like to invest your time, energy, and talent. For example, the Stock Market Index.

3. For this payoff area, identify what **improvement action** you want to initiate. For example, resist trading against the weekly trend.

4. If other people are involved, determine from whom you need to **get agreement and commitment**. For example, use your broker only for trade placement, not for advice.

5. With a large goal, **reduce its size**. For example, the goal to eliminate losses.

6. **State your goal as a measurable result with a target date and cost limitations.** For example, 'To have doubled my equity by 30 June 2014 at a cost of two hours of study each day.'

7. **Initiate an action plan**
   ▸ List the actions required to accomplish the goal. For example, learn technical analysis.
   ▸ List the immediate steps needing to be taken to get the process started. For example, spend at least two hours daily studying charts and reading trading books.

TATE ON TRADING

One of the key problems that new traders face is that they confuse their skill with the luck of having entered the market during an extraordinarily powerful bull market. All ships are lifted by a rising tide. Most new traders are incapable of acknowledging that they know very little about the markets.

Much of the day in the life of a trader is spent managing information. In trading there is no shortage of information. It is possible to track the opening and closing of all major world markets courtesy of cable television. The internet has brought the dealing desk into the home with vast information resources available via the PC. It is possible to subscribe to magazines from all around the world. You can even get the *Wall Street Journal* online as it is delivered to homes in New York.

There is a problem with all this information. It is largely irrelevant to the professional trader. None of it is provided by people who actually trade for a living (this includes stockbrokers, who are commission salespeople). New traders are unfortunately prone to trying to find as many sources of information as possible. As a consequence of this they suffer from two conditions. The first goes under the traders' euphemism of 'paralysis by analysis'. Too much information causes the trader to literally seize up and be paralysed into inactivity.

The second problem with information overload is more insidious and probably more important. Humans have some unique idiosyncrasies when it comes to processing information. The first is related to our confidence in our decision-making ability. Assume that we are trading a share called NWS, and we receive a single piece of information and we are asked to rate how confident we feel about any outcome based upon the limited information we have received. We can, for the purpose of the exercise, assign an arbitrary weighting to our confidence. Say that with one piece of information we are 10 per cent confident. If we get another piece of information our confidence may go to 20 per cent.

This is reasonable as we have doubled the information we have received so our confidence level doubles. However, if we get three sources of information our confidence level instead of going to 30 per cent will suddenly rocket to 90 per cent. Traders become disproportionately more confident with a slight increase in information.

An additional traders' quirk applies to how we process more and more information. The more information we get the more we focus on the superfluous and the irrelevant. What has been found is that traders become less accurate the more information they receive.

While it is psychologically comforting to feel that your opinions are validated by the opinions of others, there is overwhelming evidence that you will not get rich listening to the advice of others.

The new trader needs to manage the information they are receiving to ensure that they are receiving information that is only pertinent to them and is not tainted by the opinions of others. Traders need raw information, not recommendations.

Chapter 10 will help you see trading as a big problem to be solved. You really need to hear what Harry has to say here, so keep on reading...

TRADING AS A PROBLEM TO BE SOLVED

'Twenty years from now you will be more disappointed by the things that you didn't do than by the ones you did do, so throw off the bowlines, sail away from safe harbor, catch the trade winds in your sails. Explore, Dream, Discover.'

– Mark Twain

One of the greatest difficulties in attempting to solve problems is to clarify what the problem actually is.

The following model achieves such clarification and then prompts us to ask the questions that will lead us towards an answer.

Problem solving

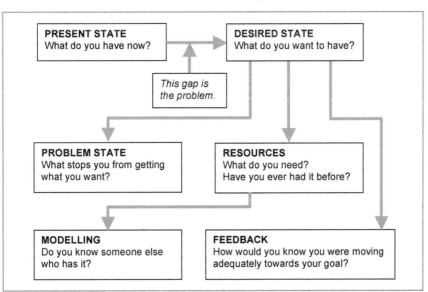

PRESENT STATE
What do you have now?

DESIRED STATE
What do you want to have?

This gap is
the problem.

PROBLEM STATE
What stops you from getting
what you want?

RESOURCES
What do you need?
Have you ever had it before?

MODELLING
Do you know someone else
who has it?

FEEDBACK
How would you know you were moving
adequately towards your goal?

Present state

To establish a starting point for problem solving, it is necessary to establish where we are at the moment. As traders, the following evaluation profile may help you achieve this. Of course, it will only do so if you answer 'yes' or 'no' honestly.

Trader evaluation profile

1. I use stop-loss orders.
2. I trade on the advice of brokers and other 'experts'.
3. I often lie awake at night worrying about my trades.
4. I ignore the 'news' and other opinions.
5. My losses create negative states of depression and self-pity within me.
6. I often fret and agonise about losses long after the trade has been concluded.
7. My profits come from closely following my trading system.
8. I am coming to believe I will never be a winning trader.
9. I study the market regularly every day.
10. I often close out my positions before my system signals tell me to do so.
11. I close out trades only when my system tells me to do so.
12. Trading is a business requiring patience plus experience.
13. I change trading systems frequently.
14. On average, my losing trades are larger than my profitable trades.
15. After a number of losing trades I reduce my trading or take a complete break.
16. I alone am fully responsible for my profits and losses.
17. Successful traders make their own decisions irrespective of other people's opinions.
18. My largest losses have been due to second-guessing my trading system.
19. Uncontrolled emotion is the chief enemy of successful speculation.
20. My trades are planned outside of market hours.
21. I do not like to have a specific trading system.
22. Traders need 'inside information' if they are to make profits in the market.
23. Fear of missing good trades prevents me taking holidays.
24. I am patient in waiting for strong entry and exit signals.
25. Several successive losses cause me to lose faith in my trading system.
26. I am slack at keeping my charting up to date.
27. I believe that I can learn to be a successful trader.
28. I often make spur-of-the-moment decisions, guided by 'gut feelings'.
29. Most trading systems can make money if money-management principles are used.
30. I frequently take large losses through hoping a poor position will improve.

Your 'Yes' or 'No' answers to these items will give you an estimate of your present position on the scale of trading excellence. The majority of successful traders would give the following answers:

1. Yes	**2.** No	**3.** No	**4.** Yes	**5.** No	**6.** No
7. Yes	**8.** No	**9.** Yes	**10.** No	**11.** Yes	**12.** Yes
13. No	**14.** No	**15.** Yes	**16.** Yes	**17.** Yes	**18.** Yes
19. Yes	**20.** Yes	**21.** No	**22.** No	**23.** No	**24.** Yes
25. No	**26.** No	**27.** Yes	**28.** No	**29.** Yes	**30.** No

If you would care to rate yourself as a trader on the basis of this profile, you could allot one point for each of your answers that agree with those given above. A score of 25 to 30 would put you in the 'outstanding trader' class, while one of 20 to 25 would certainly indicate that you employ sound trading practices. Should your score be below 20, you will need to put more work into lifting your performance. This is particularly so if you have rated yourself below 15.

Another approach to the rating of your trading skills is through the use of the following scales.

	1	2	3	4	5	
I usually trade relaxed						anxious
I usually trade focused						distracted
I usually trade confident						unsure
I usually trade with control						no control
My trading is automatic						indecisive
I trade effortlessly						with great effort
I trade feeling energised						lethargic
I trade with positive beliefs						negative
I trade with positive self-talk						negative
I find trading fun						laboured

As the ancient Greek adage puts it, 'know thyself', for this is the starting point for all self-improvement. Such self-knowledge can be improved through a comparison of your own behaviour with that of losing traders.

WHY DO MOST TRADERS LOSE?

People participating in several trading seminars in the US were asked: 'What are the most typical errors committed by traders?' The answers to this question are summarised in the following diagram:

Why do traders lose?

NO TRADING PLAN

Therefore:
- lack of confidence
- anxiety about execution
- fear of loss.

THE FIVE GREATEST BLUNDERS

1. Not taking loss at the right time.
2. Not acting on signals.
3. Closing profitable trades too soon or too late.
4. Acting on extraneous input.
5. Trading with insufficient capital.

Even the most cursory of inspections provides support for those who claim that of all the things that can go wrong in the market, most occur because of the trader, not because of the market itself or the trading system being used. In fact, the most serious of errors relate to not following trading-system rules. This raises the point made earlier. If you are not going to follow the rules, why bother to have a system?

Jake Bernstein, one of the most prolific writers about trading, believes there are five major blunders that explain why most market players lose. As he puts it, these seem to be universal among traders and investors. Fortunately, although these common errors are immensely costly, they can be rectified.

1. Failing to take a loss at the right time

This error is primarily a function of the fact that people normally find it easier to do nothing than to take action. Getting out of a position at the appropriate time requires you to do something. With a loss, this something is not pleasant, primarily because the consequences involved are negative.

An important point made by Bernstein is that failure to take losses promptly is probably due to random reinforcement. That is, sometimes we are rewarded for doing the wrong thing – breaking the rules of our system by not closing out a loss when it tells you to and then finding the market recovers to give you a profit. If this should happen several times, you are encouraged to override your system signals.

Though you may get away with 'riding out' a losing trade occasionally, in the long run you are likely to get badly hurt. That is why giving your broker a stop at the time a trade is entered is so valuable. It removes you from the market automatically, without second guessing and without having to do anything further.

Mental stops (deciding in your mind where a stop should be) don't work as well because all too frequently when our mental stop is hit we hang on longer hoping things will reverse and go our way. They rarely do. As Murphy's Law has it, anything that can go wrong will go wrong, and in the worst possible way. Every experienced trader can give examples attesting to the truth of this Law.

2. Failing to act on signals

Bernstein's second great blunder points out that by not acting on buy and sell signals generated by your trading system, you leave yourself open to many errors such as chasing the market, waiting for prices to retrace, panicking, and buying or selling too late. Of course, if you really believe in your trading system, you have no such problem.

If you are consistently ignoring or overriding your entry and exit signals, this tells you that you have no faith in your system and it is rather pointless continuing to trade it.

3. Closing out profits too soon or too late

The root cause of closing out profits too soon or too late is failure to keep to the rules of your system. So it is becoming increasingly apparent that having a system to follow and disciplining yourself to take all its signals automatically eliminates most of the blunders to which

Bernstein refers. By exercising this discipline you overcome your emotional, haphazard decision-making and replace it with a more systematic approach.

4. Listening to too many opinions

It's been said that less than 15 per cent of traders actually make any profits, and that only about a third of these achieve really significant rewards. Acting on extraneous information, even if derived from the financial 'experts', is not likely to be very helpful. Information derived from sources other than the signals generated by your trading system is often confusing and interferes with your focus. This is particularly so for the material that appears in newspapers, magazines, and news services, for most of this is either useless or quite harmful in its inaccuracy. Keep to one central point of concentration – your system – and ignore the rest.

5. Trading with insufficient capital

Attempting to trade with insufficient capital makes for a very nervous trader. Probability theory tells us that even with a system such as Chris Tate's and Louise Bedford's that may be right the majority of the time, a run of 10 consecutive losses will probably still be encountered. Fortunately, such a dismal outcome is likely to occur only once among thousands of trades. Also, taken at face value, a probability statement such as this can be very misleading when the ratio of 'average profit to average loss' is taken into account.

Still, the point is a valid one. The trader with funds that are too limited has little hope of riding out bad runs even if he or she is cutting losses short with stops. In reality, most people quit after three or four consecutive losses unless they are sufficiently capitalised.

On the other hand, the trader who begins with sufficient funds and follows a conservative money-management approach has a relatively good chance of success.

DESIRED STATE

So far we have been looking at the first question, 'What do I have now?', or the Present State. Now let's shift to the Desired State, looking at the question, 'What do I want to have?', and it is here we need to focus on what it is that the winners possess that losers do not.

Winners and losers

WINNERS	LOSERS
▸ Trade for self-knowledge as well as money.	▸ Trade out of fear of impending economic disaster or compulsive desire for market activity.
▸ Follow very specific plans and rules.	▸ Have no specific plans or rules.
▸ Learn from each trade.	▸ Rely on their "luck" changing.
▸ When wrong, use information to change themselves or their system.	▸ Have no real goals other than to make back lost funds.
▸ Are always growing.	▸ Blame others for their losses.
▸ Assume responsibility for trades.	▸ Trade for the excitement.
▸ Take carefully planned risks.	▸ Experience considerable stress.

Presumably in our Desired State we would like to possess the characteristics of top traders. These would include the following:

WHAT TOP TRADERS HAVE

Patience
Discipline
Independence
Love of the game
Emotional detachment
Willingness to take risks
Trading to win, not for excitement
Self-confidence – total belief in success
Acceptance that losing is part of the game
Responsibility for, and learning from, each trade
An effective winning strategy – a perceptual filter to fit the trader's personality

---

▷ **Patience** is said to be a virtue. For the trader it is not only a virtue but a necessity. Rushing into trades is an invitation to disaster, whereas patiently waiting for the right trade to come along is the way to success.

▷ Patience to stay with a winning position, to not close it out prematurely, is probably even more important.

▷ Following a system can be helpful if it provides clear-cut entry and exit points. Until these points arrive, you must sit tight, abstaining from making a trade. When the appropriate conditions are present, then you act.

This requires **discipline,** the most mentioned quality when top traders attempt to explain why they have been successful. You need discipline if you are to stick to the rules of your method without second-guessing.

▷ One of the main reasons why traders fail is that they think trading is easy.

▷ An **overwhelming desire and persistence to succeed as a trader** is certainly something to be desired also, as is a strong sense of **independence**. As I have mentioned earlier, successful traders base their

▷ trading decisions on their own opinions or their own systems irrespective of what others, or the 'news', might say. It is necessary to behave in this way because it is your own approach in which you must have confidence.

When interviewed by Schwager in *The New Market Wizards*, Linda Raschke put it this way: 'If you ever find yourself tempted to seek out

▷ someone else's opinion on a trade, that's usually a sure sign that you should get out of your position.' So resist the urge to seek advice.

Good traders **love the game**, for its own sake. Trading is a source of pleasure, an opportunity to play the game because of the enjoyment it generates. Yet, they do not permit the excitement of the game to carry them away. Instead, they cultivate a form of scientific detachment, distancing themselves from feelings regarding their positions.

You must accept that your thoughts are just thoughts. They are not 'you' or 'reality', yet unless you are very self-observant, you can allow them to control you.

You study your charts, for example, and see a strong entry signal but, instead of placing the trade, you decide not to do so because 'it's a bad

▷ time to trade'. Thus, you are allowing the thought that it is a 'bad time to trade', whether it has any truth or not, to override your system and thus control your behaviour. The issue here is to separate your trading system from your feelings about the trade and see it as it is – your system is telling you to enter the market.

The real secret is to see the thought 'it is a bad time to trade', then let it go. In this way you avoid becoming lost in a self-created world of fear and insecurity.

LOUISE'S THOUGHTS

The chapter you have just read is my favourite chapter of this book. Year after year I took the 'Trader Evaluation Profile' quiz, noting where I had improved and where I still needed work. If you've breezed through Harry's words, without really absorbing them or filling in the profile, I urge you to go back now and complete it.

As well as traders loving the game, as Harry has suggested, in my experience they must really *want* to succeed. With the pressures of life, sometimes it can be difficult to focus on our true heart's desires. If you ask any child what they want, usually they are able to spell out exactly what they are hoping for. They are uncannily in tune with their own emotions, hopes, and dreams.

You need to tap into this fountain of inspiration. Complete the following exercise to help you work out what is really important in your life. Don't over-think this exercise and put down something like 'World Peace'. Make it personal, selfish, and relevant to you. Complete as many 'I wants' as you can.

I want: _____

I want: _____

I want: _____

I want: _____

I want: _____

I want: _____

I want: _____

I want: _____

I want: _____

I want: _____

I want: _____

I want: _____

I want: _____

I want: _____

I want: _____

I want: _____

I want: _____

I want: _____

I want: _____

I want: _____

I really want: _____

The next chapter will help you handle stress. If you haven't confronted stress yet as a trader ... you will ... just give it time.

Harry has some more great advice for you so keep reading.

CHAPTER 11

The author fails to know that we quit a trade when using a system because no system's perfect and multiple trials and failures occur

STRESS AND THE TRADER

and for every system adjust there is a fresh set of trials that - reawaken the fear and losses occur as we trial the system

'Go confidently in the direction of your dreams.
Live the life you have imagined.'

– Henry David Thoreau

WHAT STOPS YOU?

This whole book is really an answer to this question – the third element in the problem-solving model of the previous chapter.

We stop ourselves. Our own thinking and lack of emotional discipline can stop us in our tracks. In fact, it can seem as if our lives are one long obstacle course, with ourselves as the chief obstacles.

Stress is a major factor. It can disrupt your emotional balance and rattle you to your core.

But what *is* stress? When people are asked this question, their answers indicate they usually have a pretty clear idea of what they are talking about. They mention various physiological and psychological symptoms, such as headaches, stomach upsets, insomnia, irritability, and poor concentration. When you're experiencing stress, you may even feel an inability to cope, a lack of control over yourself, and a general feeling of unease. It greatly impairs our capacity to think creatively.

Traders facing large losses, particularly if these were the result of ignoring proven system rules, experience this feeling. When trading becomes 'distressful' in this way, traders are unable to see the full range of alternatives available to them. They lose flexibility and their thinking tends to become rigid. This is unlikely to be beneficial to their trading.

Conversely, though we rarely think of it this way, demands and pressures can lead us in the opposite direction – to a state of 'eustress'. This is the stress of winning and achievement. It's the sense of exhilaration you experience when you are meeting and overcoming challenges.

Traders often feel this 'eustress' when they plan and execute a trade which develops in the way they anticipated, so that significant profits are produced. We welcome such stress both for the positive feelings it brings and for the flexible, creative thinking it encourages.

When traders get together, they usually speak of the methods they are using in their ongoing battle with the market. I recall one relatively experienced trader, Gary, talking of the stress he felt due to losing even when he was 'doing the right thing'.

Gary's story

Gary was using a system producing about a 60 per cent success rate, yet was being stopped out again and again, despite his analysis being proven correct (as the market moved in the direction he had predicted). This is not an unusual scenario.

When Gary told me about his situation in a seminar I was running, I could see many of the traders who were listening nodding their heads in agreement. Gary then outlined his current trading strategy. One of the main points he decided to utilise was the use of looser stops.

Plus, Gary was fixated on his 'hit rate', and proud of his '60 per cent correct' track record. This was a dangerous mindset. It's not how many trades you get 'right', it's the total profit you make per trade that will make you money overall.

In fact, the Turtles, who are one of the most successful trading groups in the entire world, only maintain a success hit rate of around 35 per cent. The reason they're so successful is they cut their losses quickly but pyramid aggressively into their winning trades. This ensures that substantial profits are accrued for the 35 per cent of trades that do result in a win.

For me, Gary's experience served to emphasise a very important point about trading and about life in general. Just as there is no one 'right way' to trade, there is no one 'right way' to live your life successfully. Each of us has to find our own best way, one that suits us as individuals. To trade successfully, you must find an approach that suits your personality so you can feel comfortable. This may not be the way the 'experts' tell you, but it is still likely to work best for you.

You are not going to be able to achieve this emotional discipline with an approach that, no matter how 'correct', makes you feel uncomfortable. However, when you do find a way of trading that seems to fit your personality, you are likely to be less stressed and therefore more in control of yourself psychologically. In fact, how you handle stress in your life will make a tremendous difference to your success or otherwise as a trader.

STRESS IS A FUNCTION OF YOUR PERCEPTION

In my Stress Management seminars, I often begin by asking participants to complete the following exercise.

STRESS ANALYSIS EXERCISE

1. List the things that produce distress in your life.

2. For each of these note:
    WHO is involved in your distress?
    WHERE does this distress occur?
    HOW FREQUENTLY does this distress occur?
    Do you feel as if you have any CONTROL in the situation?

3. Put a * next to those distressful situations to which there seems to be a remedy.

4. Put a ** next to the three items you would most like to resolve.

The most important outcome of this exercise is that it shows participants that they are largely responsible for their own stress. Apart from flood, famine, and war, we do create virtually all our stress by the way we choose to think about the events that occur in our lives. This is not easy to admit. Nor is it easy to accept responsibility for doing something about it. In fact, it has been said, somewhat cynically, that one of the main reasons for marriage is that we need someone to blame so we can avoid taking responsibility for our own actions.

Stress is often assumed to be something external, malignantly waiting to pounce upon us, rather than it being something internal, a function of how we choose to react to the events in our lives. Again, it comes back to a matter of separating 'what is', that which actually occurs, from what we are adding to 'what is'. Let us look at an example.

Is your boss out to get you?

At work, your boss brushes past you without answering your 'good morning'. This is the 'what is' – the event that actually occurred.

Now, it is quite likely you will spend the rest of the morning worrying about why your boss is displeased with you. Has he found out about your latest blunder? Why is he no longer friendly?

You are creating your own stress about this situation. You don't know why your boss is off-hand, and all your worrying and fretting is not going to change anything. In fact, it probably has nothing to do with you at all. Perhaps he has had harsh words with his wife, or the traffic has been bad, or his stomach is upset. You just don't know. Yet, you impose great stress upon yourself by adding fears, anxiety, and frustration because of the way you interpret his actions.

This scenario, repeated on many occasions, is likely to create a chronic stress problem; one you will blame on your boss, the work environment, your spouse, the media, or something else. Rarely will you look inside yourself to discover the real reason why you feel so strung out. If you do accept your own responsibility for your state, the solution is within your grasp.

Take more control over the way you think, or you will be at the mercy of any thought that comes into your mind. If you think thoughts such as, 'I will not trade until I am sure I will not make a loss', and act as if this is true, you impose great pressure upon yourself. This thought pattern virtually ensures that you will never actually trade.

Similarly, thoughts like 'the market is out to get me' or 'nothing ever seems to work out the way it does with my paper trades' create stress within you if you actually allow yourself to believe them. But you don't have to.

Thousands of thoughts come into your mind every day. They may be true, partly true, false, or totally irrelevant. However, they can exert an influence over your life if you accept they are true and act accordingly.

If you accept as true that the market is out to get you, you will feel resentful, frustrated, and stressed. But the market does not care about you as an individual. It simply is. So your thought is wrong. You have allowed a false thought to make you stressed. If you can give a thought the power to do this to you, you can also withdraw this power.

Imagine you are sitting in a cave watching a waterfall outside the entrance. Think of this cascade as your thoughts, a constant, never-ending torrent, from which you are separated by being back in the cave. You watch the thoughts flowing past at a distance but, just as you don't have to get wet in the waterfall until you choose to do so, similarly you don't have to involve yourself in your thoughts unless you want to. Why choose to involve yourself in thoughts that will create stress within you unless, by so doing, you can improve upon your situation? This is rarely the case. Usually all you achieve by worrying and fretting is to make yourself and everyone around you feel bad.

When is stress harmful?

Stress is disadvantageous for you as a trader if it interferes with your emotional separation from the markets. Separation allows you to step back and watch your thoughts about trading before you decide which ones you will allow to influence you. There are many unknowns in trading, such as:

▸ Should I stay with my system after four losing trades?

▸ Should I wait a little longer and thereby miss a profitable trade, or jump in now?

▸ Should I use a wide or a tight stop?

For each of these questions and countless others raised daily when trading, there is no correct answer.

Regardless of the choice made, the outcome of that specific decision is unknown. Stress arises when one has to make a decision between two or more choices and the outcome of either choice is unknown; or, having made a decision, stress arises when you have no control over the outcome. Since each of the above questions requires a decision, and since the decision is based on unknown outcomes, a trader continuously faces stress.

Some people find this stimulating, others find it distressing. The actual event is the same – it is the perception of the event that differs.

Some ways of handling distress

One method of improving this situation is to take an **Ultradian break**. Research evidence indicates that approximately every hour and a half, human beings experience a sort of 'let-down' for about a quarter-of-an-hour. During this time we tend to fumble over words, make mistakes, find it difficult to concentrate, and become more forgetful. If you attempt to work through these 'let-down' periods, you will become increasingly stressed so that your data analysis and trading decisions will become more fraught with error.

During this time, as you recognise it occurring, it is helpful to lie down or relax in a chair. Notice which part of your body feels most comfortable, and then relax into that comfort, which will spread auto-matically to other parts of your body. Then tune into your breathing, heartbeat, or pulse. Feel its rhythm without attempting to change it.

Simply go with it, then let your mind wander to a favourite fantasy, image, or restful idea. Alternatively you might like to use this peace-ful time to review some real-life experiences that are comforting and positive.

Another straight-forward approach to the alleviation of stress is the Six B Plan.

The Six B Plan

Breathe	- take two deep breaths.
Beam	- smile broadly.
Body relax	- let go tension in jaw, brow, neck, shoulders, stomach, hands.
Body balance	- stand tall, look up, smile, stretch arms up.
Brain	- talk to yourself in positive, encouraging, supportive ways.
Back	- step back, detaching yourself from thoughts and feelings. See them pass like movies on a screen.

In his book *Beyond the Investor's Quotient*, Bernstein also had some thoughts about how stress might be handled more effectively. His pre-scription includes the following steps:

▸ Stop excessive stress before it starts. For example, take regular vacations, work a reasonable number of hours per day.

▸ Don't try to trade every market. Attempt to trade in specific markets. Try to become an expert in a few things.

▸ Don't try to catch every move. It is not possible to catch every daily, weekly, or monthly move. Specialise in one or two time perspectives.

▸ Don't set your goals too high. For example, first focus on avoiding losses, then on increasing equity, and lastly on making a lot of money. Too many people try to do it the other way round.

▸ Don't take the market home with you. Begin each day fresh.

▸ Find a way to vent stress and pressure. For example, regular physical exercise.

So the message is clear. Do everything you can to reduce the level of stress in your life and your trading.

However, this may be easier said than done. Many of us are very poor at identifying our stress level, not even realising that excessive stress is the cause of our emotional distress. The following scale might help you here:

The stress test

Look back over the past six months. Have you noticed any of these changes in yourself or in the world around you? Assign each one a score from 1 to 5 – 1 for 'no change' to 5 for 'great change'.

1. Do you tire more easily? Do you feel fatigued rather than energetic?
2. Are people annoying you by remarking how tired you look?
3. Do you seem to be working harder and harder, but accomplishing less?
4. Are you increasingly cynical and disenchanted?
5. Do you find that criticism of others arises more easily to your lips than praise?
6. Are you often invaded by a sadness you can't explain?
7. Are you forgetting (appointments, deadlines, personal possessions)?
8. Are you increasingly irritable? More disappointed in the people around you?
9. Are you seeing close friends and family members less frequently? Have you recently had a chat about nothing in particular with an adult or child you love?
10. Are you too busy to do routine things like make phone calls, go to the hairdresser, or send birthday cards?
11. Do you frequently have backaches, other pains, headaches, or colds that simply will not go away?
12. Do you feel at a loss when the activity of the day comes to a halt?
13. Do you find jokes about yourself so hurtful it makes it hard to laugh?
14. Does sex seem like more trouble than it is worth?
15. Is joy elusive?
16. Do you have little to say to people who are not involved in your home or your work?

▶ If you score over 35, life is not as pleasant as it could be. Sit down and think about how you could reduce your distress – and be kinder to yourself.
▶ If you score over 65, you may need to consult a doctor for professional counseling.

OTHER APPROACHES TO MANAGING STRESS

I work a lot with people in very stressful situations, such as police officers, teachers, nurses, and, of course, traders. However, because stress is a matter of perception, many of these individuals experience little distress. They really enjoy the challenge of the work they do. On the other hand, many do react badly to the pressures of their work.

When such people consult a doctor for advice, one piece of advice they may receive is to take a holiday. This is certainly likely to be helpful, as we usually relax on holidays and shed much of our stress, but it is often not possible for us to take this advice.

Fortunately, the 'mental holiday' can provide an excellent substitute.

Take a mental holiday

To take a very enjoyable holiday in your mind means setting aside perhaps 10 to 20 minutes in order to turn off the world for a while and enter into a little world of your own creation. Perhaps you could imagine passing through a door to find a special place waiting for you, a place where you will feel happy, contented, and tranquil. Beaches, gardens, warm beds, and lovely rooms are popular choices. As you close the door, you shut out the world and its disturbances. Your special place is a sanctuary, an oasis of self-created calm in a busy, busy world.

Should you feel definite physical tension gazing at the computer screen, it is useful to check four key areas of your body. Often, when we are concentrating hard, we tense many more of our muscles than is really required by the task in which we are engaged. When drawing or writing, for example, though you have to hold the pen firmly and make the appropriate movements, you have no need to clench your jaw, furrow your brow, clench the hand not being used for writing, or tighten the stomach muscles. Yet, if you check on yourself, there is a reasonable chance that you will be doing some or all of these things. Release this physical stress by deliberately loosening your jaw, let your teeth part a little, smooth out your forehead, relax your hand, and let go of the tension in your stomach. If you do this from time to time your work will be more productive, for longer, and you will feel far fresher when you finish.

Time management counts

Your life will also proceed more smoothly if you devote some attention to the way in which you manage your time. A main source of stress in our lives is the misuse of this vital resource. If we use time well, our work, be it trading or anything else, becomes increasingly efficient, hopefully releasing sufficient time for much-needed relaxation activities. However, if we use time poorly, we are under constant pressure, a pressure that can totally destroy our ability to achieve the trading results we deserve.

One of the simplest, and yet one of the most effective, of all time management techniques is to write down, in order of importance, three things you want most to accomplish the next day as you study your charts and data. This is usually done when you have finished your work for the night. In the area you use for your trading analysis, clear everything else out of sight except for the materials necessary to do the first priority item.

This removes your biggest problem – that of getting started. The next day, you know precisely what your first task is to be. It is all there open in front of you, ready for you to begin. You know you are likely to be interrupted occasionally but, each time, return to that number one priority until you have finished it. Then you cross it off your list, which provides a real sense of satisfaction, and remove everything from sight except materials needed for the second priority task, and make a start on that. This is the essence of time management; the creation of a sense of purpose and a sense of direction.

A sense of direction is vital because we are often unclear about what is really important to us. As a result, we spend a lot of time doing things that give us no sense of satisfaction or fulfillment.

There is, fortunately, a way to find out if this is indeed the case. Use a Time Log. For a week, keep a detailed record of how you spend every moment. At the end of the week, when you look at how you have used your time, you will probably become very aware that the 80/20 concept is alive and well.

If we arrange, in order of importance, everything we have to do, 80 per cent of the value is likely to come from only 20 per cent of the things we have listed. This is where the Time Log can be so helpful in identifying what we actually do – 80 per cent of our satisfaction, enjoyment, and sense of accomplishment usually comes from 20 per cent of the things listed in our log.

Ideally we should concentrate our efforts upon those relatively few tasks that are likely to yield most value to us in terms of furtherance of our aims. If we complete these high-yielding tasks, it will not matter very much if the other 80 per cent is left undone. The secret of good time management is to eliminate as many of these non-productive tasks as possible and to use the time thus gained in doing those things that are producing the most value, enjoyment, and sense of fulfillment.

Avoid trivia at all cost

Adoption of the 80/20 rule is one way, then, we can avoid becoming bogged down in an ocean of trivia. Extending the rule further will lead to increased conservation of time and energy for it suggests that 80 per cent of the value derived from a specific task is gained in the first 20 per cent of the work time spent upon it. Being a perfectionist, then, would not seem to be very advantageous behaviour. We would be working far too hard for minimum benefits. Once the initial gains have been derived, we would receive increasingly diminishing rewards for our further efforts. However, there are some tasks where much of the value does come in the last 20 per cent of effort. In such cases, the perfection-ist approach makes good sense in that it is an appropriate allocation of time.

Stay on track

There is a need to remind yourself frequently about your main goals so that you make sure you are doing something every day to move towards their attainment. Perhaps you could write them out on cards that you place all around the house and in other areas where you are likely to see them. You can even tuck a little card under the wristband of your watch so that on every occasion you check the time seeing the card prompts you to think about your main objective.

Take each day as a fresh start; a new beginning, for you can consider every day as if it were a new life. Unfortunately many people persist in looking into the past and thinking, 'Oh, I've messed up this type of trade in the past ...' or they project into the future, 'This is going to be a very difficult trade ...'. The beautiful thing about the future is that it only comes one day at a time. Each time you start again in the morning you have been given this gift of a new life; a fresh set of opportunities.

Pair your activities

Another chance to screw up!

Sometimes you will feel tired, and concentrating on your trading materials just seems too much of a chore. One way of easing the strain somewhat is to pair tasks. So, instead of telling yourself you do not have enough energy to do any work on your charts, try this thought instead: 'What I'm going to do is half an hour on the charts, then I'm going to immediately reward myself with something I really like doing.' Having done this, study your trading materials for another three-quarters of an hour and reward yourself again.

This is grandma's remedy – you don't get to eat your dessert until you eat your vegetables. Very sensible advice for, should you eat the dessert first, you will never get around to those vegetables. If you adopt this pattern of constantly pairing activities, you will find you not only achieve more but you will be enjoying what you are doing because of the steady flow of rewards it brings.

Perhaps the reason why so many of us use our time inefficiently is our lack of clarity about our goals. If we are not clear about what we want to achieve, it is virtually impossible to give priority to those activities that are moving us towards our objectives. A way to clarify goals is through the quick-list technique. Simply write down, off the 'top of your head', the three things you want most in your life at this particular moment. Put the list away, and next week, at about the same time, repeat the procedure. Continue this process until, after six weeks, you have six lists. When you look at these six lists you will probably see a definite pattern, a repetition of the same items. These are your goals.

It is useful to repeat the process every six months as our goals do tend to change, often without us knowing that they are doing so. If we have not realised this, we continue doing things that are no longer of real value, for they are moving us towards goals that are no longer of any personal importance. When first involving ourselves in trading, for example, our first goal might be to learn the skills necessary for survival in the market without taking losses that would wipe us out. As we gradually acquire these skills, this very wise goal of capital preservation, though still present, might be superseded by the goal of steadily increasing our equity. Once this has taken place satisfactorily, the next goal might be one of making large amounts of money.

AAABC'S OF STRESS CONTROL

The same situation evokes different responses depending on the attitude of those involved in the situation. For traders, feelings of powerlessness can be an issue as they come face to face with the reality that they can exert no control over the market. Poor-quality relationships can be present, with trading being used as a retreat from handling difficulties in communication. Role conflicts can emerge, with so much time being spent on trading that there is no time left for family interaction.

Use the methods described earlier in this chapter to handle distress-provoking situations such as these, or perhaps the AAAbc's of stress management which follow might provide you with some inspiration.

Alter – remove the source of stress by changing something. For example, make better use of time.

Avoid – remove yourself from the stressful situation. For example, learn to say 'no'.

Accept – equip yourself physically and mentally to manage stress.

Build resistance – increase your capacity to tolerate stress physically. For example, proper diet, regular exercise, relaxation techniques.

Bolster mental resistance. For example, clarify your goals, use success imagery.

Strengthen social resistance – e.g. build and maintain support systems. Strengthen spiritual resistance – e.g. pray.

Change – the way you perceive the situation or yourself. For example, change unrealistic expectations and irrational beliefs; reframe situations positively.

By adopting the particular methods that suit you, you will be able to reduce your distress. To some extent this will take place through inhibiting the biochemical component of stress, such as the release of anxiety-provoking hormones.

Practise of the techniques of stress control, and indeed the other techniques outlined throughout this book, will help you towards more positive reactions to stress, ones that will enhance your ability to make better decisions rather than ones that undermine your clarity of judgement.

TATE ON TRADING

Louise here. I'm hijacking Chris's section temporarily. No discussion of mindset would be complete without hearing Chris Tate's views. I've included an excerpt of an interview with Chris so you can compare the way you think with how a professional trader views the world.

If you're seriously after a gigantic financial breakthrough in your own trading results, you need to read carefully absolutely everything that Chris has to say.

What was your trading approach initially and how did it change over time?

Like everyone, I took a fundamental approach and thought that it was important to understand the fundamentals of the companies whose stocks I was planning to trade.

As a scientist, I had thought that building a large pool of knowledge would give me an edge, but I found out early on in my career that fundamental analysis did not necessarily pan out. The markets were not consistent with that paradigm.

I gradually shifted toward being more technical and much more mechanical in the way I approached trading.

Did your training as a scientist help in any way?

I suppose one of the joys of having been trained as a scientist is an understanding of the scientific method.

In many ways, I approached trading as a very large experiment. I continually formed hypotheses of the way I behaved and the way the markets behaved, and literally tested each one with my own money. I tried to weed out the unsupported hypotheses, but in the end, I concluded that many of my ideas had no utility whatsoever.

They were of no use at all?

Largely. Understanding the fundamentals of the company had no utility. That realisation led me toward looking at group dynamics, group theory, decision-making, and how individuals behaved as a herd.

More importantly, I started looking more closely at how I behaved in response to the markets. The markets provide a feedback system. What I found most important was the way I perceived the changes in the market and the way I reacted to these changes.

How did you react to changes in the markets? What psychological obstacles did you overcome?

I went through the classic problems that all traders go through, such as taking advice from others. I tended to believe that those who gave advice knew what they talking about, when they did not.

It feels good to give up responsibility to a higher authority, but that doesn't work well.

I used to think it was a good idea to average down, which isn't a good idea. I learned that money management was a key to consistent trading. When I first traded, I was very aggressive, and very much driven by testosterone. Testosterone tends to make you dumb. It clouds the perceptions you need for trading.

Do you feel that there's a lot more subjectivity in technical analysis than a scientist would prefer?

There is, but what you have to fall back on are a few very robust ideas. I must admit, the only things I have learned over the past 30 years of any utility whatsoever are three simple maxims:

1   If the market is trending up, you buy.

2   If the market is trending down, you sell.

3   Always manage your risk.

I have come full circle from not knowing a lot, but being desperate to know everything, to having passed through that part of the curve where I felt I did know everything. I've now come back to taking a very simple approach.

Do you think traders make trading more difficult than it should be?

Most people who engage in technical analysis often cloud what's going on with an arsenal of tools that are really quite irrelevant. Oscillators or indicators fall into two types: they indicate either trend or sentiment.

Many traders try to make it more complex than that. They add layers of complexity that are analogous to a Russian Babushka Doll, where you pull the top off one doll, and there is another one underneath it. You pull that top off again, and there is yet another one, and it goes on in an endless cycle.

Continually overlaying price with an enormous battery of information is like loading one doll on top of another. Doing so obscures the actual price.

We seem to go through a cycling of very trendy indicators. They come into vogue for some time and they shift out. This goes on and on. For example, someone will make a variation on a moving average and that will become the next hot thing for a year or so, but then we move on and find something new and trendy.

There is a dramatic tendency to try to obscure what the market is telling you and a desperate and probably futile attempt to bring predictability and order to what is essentially a chaotic system.

Why do you think that is?

I think it is because we live in a rules-based society. People struggle with the fact that markets are largely unknown in what they will do.

The markets go in the direction they want to go irrespective of where you want them to go. All of this direction of energy toward better prediction is just a basic human desire to find order, but we can't actually bring order to a chaotic system. We are really just passengers riding the market. We have to go where the market takes us.

We have to go where the market takes us?

We really do. An analogy I like to use is to say that trading and the markets are similar to surfing.

A surfer tries to look for a good wave to ride. You go out into the water and put yourself on the surfboard and wait for a good wave. There are many different kinds of waves.

There are waves that will take you all the way to the shore. Other waves are merely small perturbations that just simply lift the board a little bit and get you nowhere. Occasionally, you will encounter a wave that will pick you up and slam you into the sand, and there are those rare ultimate waves that you will tell your friends about for years to come.

You can't predict when the next wave will arrive, and you can't predict what the next wave will be like. That's impossible.

However, you can predict that there will definitely be another wave, and that when you encounter it, you will have your surfboard pointed in the right direction to take advantage of it.

One doesn't need predictability. It's quite possible to look out at the ocean from the beach for the entire day and see nothing happen. On other days, it is constant activity from the moment you hit the water until the moment you drag yourself out very cold and exhausted at the end of the day.

Trading is just like that.

All we can do is merely equip ourselves with the skills we need to catch the next wave. One doesn't know when the wave will come or how big it will be. But, one knows a wave will arrive eventually, and when it does, one needs to be ready to take advantage of it.

Is trading more art than science?

It is important to remember that money management rules are key.

One must stick with money management, which engenders survivability. Your method must have a survivability element so that if you literally wished to select stocks by throwing darts at a board, you would continue to survive in market to market. The longer you survive, the more chance you have of making money. The more money you have, the longer you survive.

The longer you survive, the more money you make. A cascade occurs.

With that said, there is another aspect to trading. One must have a set of rules in order to identify a trading setup. These rules are more arbitrary than money-management rules.

A stock can follow one of many possible patterns out of the entire universe of patterns. Sometimes the price action will mimic your rules, other times it will not. The trick is to be able to accurately identify when a pattern mimics your rules and take advantage of that opportunity.

What specific money-management strategies do you use?

Mine are really quite simple. I simply adopt a minimal percentage risk, such as 1 per cent. I use a volatility-based, efficient sizing methodology, which is average true range. It also has a built-in pyramiding component and a profit reinvestment component. It's really quite simple.

I subscribe to a philosophy put forth by Leon Lederman who won the 1988 Nobel Prize for Physics. He postulated that if an idea is too long to fit on a T-shirt, then it's probably wrong. It's really quite simple. It's not rocket science. I think many people are often extraordinarily disappointed that trading isn't rocket science. Having a Nobel Prize and an IQ of 190 doesn't guarantee that you will be able to trade.

Right. In *Market Wizards*, Tom Baldwin said, 'The smarter you are, the dumber you are; the more you know the worse it is for you.'

That's probably true. There are probably very few rocket science–type traders in the world.

I think William Eckhardt is an exception. He comes from an academic mathematical background. But, even if you look at his method, it is very robust. The statistics behind it are very robust.

What are some of the psychological issues that traders must overcome?

I think that humans are not programmed very well for success. I can only speak from the viewpoint of my own cultural background, and I don't know if you have the same cultural approach in the United States. Here in Australia, we have an idea called the Tall Poppy Syndrome.

If you are a tall poppy and you stand out above other people, you need a large harvester to come along and cut your head off, so that you are the same height as everyone else. I think that reflects people's deep subconscious desire to be uniform. There is a natural herd instinct to be uniform and not stand out.

Going against the tide is very difficult for people. That's to be expected because humans, like other primates, are herd based.

What are some other psychological issues?

There is also a desire for self-sabotage in people. I'm a great fan of Jungian psychology, especially the concept of the shadow. One needs to come to terms with the shadow, and you need to come to terms with how your subconscious drives behaviour. This is something that all traders must go through.

[Editor's note: In Jungian psychology, the shadow is an archetype passed on genetically across the generations. It consists of the animal instincts that humans have inherited in their evolution from lower forms of life. Jung believed that healthy individuals must integrate the good and bad aspects of themselves.]

Real trading doesn't actually occur in the markets. The markets are merely a technological aggregation that we put together to facilitate our trading.

Trading actually goes on between your ears, and as such, it's necessary to examine what goes on between your ears. Such an examination is necessary in order to make significant progress. This is true of any profession that requires high performance.

For example, if you look at the top 10 tennis players in world, they have almost identical backgrounds, yet there is always one person who is number one. That difference surely must come down to the way they think, the way they perceive themselves, their freedom of thought, and the freedom of action that they have. Whether it is subconscious, intuitive, or a true conscious understanding, traders must be aware of elements of their subconscious that will attempt to hold them back.

Many traders seem to secretly believe that trading is not a legitimate profession because it is not like a traditional job.

No, it's not. I think that's a function of a clash with traditional ideas, such as the Protestant work ethic. Work has a certain tone and tenor to it. There is a traditional notion that suffering and toil are good for you, in some sort of strange way. Trading does not fulfil those criteria. This causes a tension between those who hold on to traditional notions of work and those who have become traders.

The tension prevents people from wanting to move forward because it's easier to remain part of the general population, part of your family, or part of your ethnic group. I have found that I've struggled with this tension myself and others have told me they have also.

People who win tens of millions of dollars in the lottery seem to go through a progression that is pertinent to understanding this issue. They acquire a great deal of wealth, their lifestyle changes, and they become quite acquisitive in buying things, but after five years or so, they seem to be back to where they started from.

This may happen because as they move through this progression, they have such enormous tension within themselves, and such great difficulty and friction, that they subconsciously behave in ways that bring them back to an environment where they felt more comfortable. The environment in which they are generally more comfortable is the one in which they were socialised. It is hard to break away from it.

Traders move through a similar progression.

They trade to a certain level, and then repeatedly explode and come back. A wonderful prototype of someone who went through this progression is Jesse Livermore. He had the capacity to literally take two beans and a loaf of bread and trade them into a massive fortune. He would trade, explode, and come back, trade, explode and come back, and so on. Now, eventually he experienced terrible consequences in that he committed suicide.

That's a terrible endpoint to the journey, but for most people self-sabotage simply brings them back to where they were when they started, a point where they feel most comfortable.

In a Jungian sense, do you believe that humans have an innate motive for self-sabotage?

Yes, very much so. I think there is a complete lack of understanding about the shadow parts of people's character that causes them to do things that are not in their best interests.

Successful traders, in contrast, generally see the world in a balanced way, and have a unified view of the world. They have been able to integrate the shadow's self-sabotaging motives with other aspects of their personality. By doing so they have removed the potential for total destruction. It seems to be a theme that traders get to a certain size, something happens, and they eventually blow up. Very well known traders have reached a critical mass, and then something happens. There seems to be a short-circuiting.

Did you have the equivalent of blowing out your account a couple times?

The quick answer to that would be 'yes'.

Did you come upon this Jungian explanation while trying to figure out why?

Yes, this approach has really taken hold personally in the last 10 years. It developed while a lot of events coalesced in my life simultaneously. I had to sit down and think about how I had arrived at this point, why I was there, and how I was going to move on. I think that I had a little bit of an inherent advantage because of my background as a scientist.

In addition, Asian culture had influenced my philosophical and spiritual beliefs at an early age. My spiritual beliefs are different from Western spiritual beliefs. It is based upon the individual. The individual makes himself or herself aware, and decides how he or she fits into the big scheme of things.

Western spirituality, in contrast, is often based on the power structure the church, which tells how and where people fit into the world. Asian spiritual beliefs are directed towards the individual. My guiding philosophy is that people are always where they are in their life because of a series of circumstances that they have conspired to generate.

Now whether they do that subconsciously or consciously doesn't matter, because the end result is the same. What is more important is how you arrived at that point and how you move on.

One must realise that you got yourself to that point. It is a watershed moment, a moment in which you decide what the next step will be.

What goes on in your life from that point on is a function of what happens there and then, and I think self-realisation is something that takes time and a great deal of effort.

What do you mean by self-realisation?

One can distinguish between a shallow 'pop psychology' sort of motivation and motivation resulting from true self-realisation. In Australia, there are trading coaches who I see as merely 'professional presenters'. They take an extremely motivational, yet shallow, approach to teaching people how to trade. Their seminars involve listening to loud music, group hugs, or breaking boards as in martial arts.

I find that kind of motivational approach very unsophisticated because it doesn't compel the individual to make a pivot shift in his or her psyche, nor does it bring a self-realisation as to where they are. Their idea of increasing motivation is like giving two year olds too much sugar and caffeine, and having them run around all afternoon in a hyperactive state until they fall in the corner in tears.

These people do the same thing.

A sharp distinction needs to be made between the childish 'pop psychology' sort of motivation, and the big change inspiration that self-awareness brings. It's very hard to get people to that point of self-awareness and inspiration because it's often quite uncomfortable and painful. Whereas shallow and transitory motivation makes you feel happier because you had a big hug with a stranger, heard some loud music, gave each other a massage, or successfully walked over hot coals, the motivation resulting from life-changing events is more permanent.

Life-changing events for traders are much deeper, more personal, and result in a more powerful understanding than these shallow events.

If people are motivated by higher order needs, then why do you continue to trade? It seems as if you have enough money?

That's an exceptionally good question. I think it falls back to the notion of how much is enough? That's the really deep question. I've gone through phases in my life where I've actually given away all of my possessions because I no longer viewed money as an entity in and of itself for my life. But, that has long past. These days, my longer term trading activities concern wealth maintenance. I'm now motivated to pursue other activities as well. I focus on trading Mentor Programs and the charities I support. Trading is now a means to an end to do other things.

Once you reach a certain point in your life, money and the pursuit of possessions actually loses its attractiveness. The money no longer means anything to you. I have friends who judge themselves by what car they drive, which I view as unfortunate.

I feel sort of depressed on their behalf that the external possessions that make them feel important guide their sense of self-worth. The pursuit of money really doesn't 'float my boat'. It doesn't do anything for me. So now, I'm more motivated to teach and do other things that give my life meaning in that they help other people.

I'm a great believer that when you have been blessed with privilege and luck, it is one's obligation to do something with the gifts you have been given. As providence has smiled upon you, you should do something to assist others for whom these things have not been as easy or that the door has not opened in quite the right way.

It is incumbent upon people to actually do that, and I think it's quite selfish and childish when people don't look beyond the bounds of their own lives to assist others.

When you first got involved in trading, did you consider how the wealth you achieved could be used to help you change society? Was that always a motivation in the back of your mind?

Yes. I've never been a 'money person'. Initially, I went through a very acquisitive phase, when I first started and found success, but that didn't last very long. I actually find wealth really boring, and difficult to manage and maintain.

It becomes a very mechanical thing. Having a large account to trade becomes a mechanical thing, and many people who take up trading do so in the belief that they will swap one job for something different. But, if they don't actually have the understanding that they take up trading to change, all they simply have done is traded one job for another job. There is no change. All that changes is your working conditions. You now work from home instead of going to the office.

You're now directly responsible for most of your decisions, as opposed to being part of a hierarchy, but you have still just swapped one job for another.

There's been no spiritual change and no change in your lifestyle. You don't use your additional freedom to spend more time with your family or do anything of value whatsoever.

Right, so values are at the heart of your motivation?

I think values should be at the heart of everyone's motivation.

Now, having said that, it is somewhat of an idealistic statement, but I actually think that success is easier to achieve if it's actually value driven, rather than simply being a loose acquisition of rules that really bridges to the simple statement that you're going to screw everyone around you. I don't think that such a viewpoint is sustainable.

There is a logic that says there is always someone bigger and nastier than you, and one day, if you're not careful, you'll actually meet him or her. And if you have a completely amoral, non-spiritually driven approach to life, I think you will run into that bigger and nastier person much sooner than you might think. That's the way the world is. It relates to the idea of karma. The universe tries to balance itself out. It is easier and much more rewarding to do good things.

Keep reading to discover how to work out your next steps so that you can achieve trading success ...

CHAPTER 12

YOUR NEXT STEP

'Man is not disturbed by events, but by the view he takes of them.'

– Epictetus

STEPS TO SUCCESSFUL TRADING

In *The Disciplined Trader*, and his later book *Trading in the Zone*, Mark Douglas has outlined what he believes is necessary if one is to become a successful trader. I'd like to discuss these steps here.

1. Stay focused on learning

The first of his steps to success is staying focused on learning what is needed to become an excellent trader, rather than on making money. Adoption of this viewpoint means that there is no such thing as mistakes, only learning opportunities. Further, because the markets are always there, always moving, always providing opportunities, there can be no such thing as a missed opportunity. If there is a situation you do not make the most of, well there will be another chance shortly. Yet, as Douglas puts it:

> Except for the inability to accept a loss, there isn't anything that has the potential to cause more psychological damage than a belief in missed opportunities. Missed opportunities are trades that would have always turned out perfectly because they only occurred in our minds, where we can make anything be as we want it to be.

Having a perspective like this condemns you to emotional turmoil. Conversely, when you trade from the position that mistakes don't exist and that it is impossible to miss opportunities, you are no longer compelled to do something, anything, such as getting into trades too early or too late. It helps, in this regard, to set aside some money for the purpose of learning how to trade. Use this money for practice, providing the opportunity to learn some needed skill in a more realistic manner than if you simply paper traded.

2. Watch how you handle losses

With every trade you make, decide, before entry, the point at which the market is telling you that the trade no longer represents a profitable opportunity. Unless you accept that some losses are inevitable, and, in fact, you go into every trade with a 'Plan B' in place to manage losses, you are unlikely to become a successful trader. Until you have this acceptance, fear will be your constant companion.

As soon as you perceive the market telling you that you are wrong, exit the losing trades. Train yourself to behave in this way so that it becomes an automatic reaction, carried out without you even thinking about it. By predefining how great a loss you will permit, and exiting if this point is reached, you increase the probability that you will learn how best to let your profits grow.

3. Keep it simple

A third step likely to increase trading success involves becoming an expert in a single market behaviour that repeats itself with some degree of frequency. This means following a simple mechanical trading system based on a particular pattern that you are able to identify on a chart, then practising with many charts until you are totally familiar with every aspect of the system.

Don't be seduced into exploring other approaches until you feel you have real mastery over a simple trading system. Once you have this confidence, gradually expand your repertoire as you investigate other patterns of market behaviour. If you do follow this concept of starting small and simple, rather than the more complicated approach of looking at many different systems and indicators at the same time, you will find you become increasingly confident.

4. Learn to be objective

This is the primary message of this book.

You will know that you have achieved such a state when, as Mark Douglas puts it:

- you feel no pressure pushing you to do anything
- you trade without fear
- there is no right or wrong
- you recognise that as this is what the market is telling me, this is what I do
- you can observe the market as if you were not holding a position even when you are
- you are not focused on how much money you may or may not make, but upon the structure of the market itself.

To stay objective, analyse the market, and estimate the probabilities of the possible scenarios taking place. Decide in advance what you will do in each of these situations. Should none of your scenarios follow the course you anticipated, then get out. Release yourself from the need to be right. Accept that it is the market that is always right, not yourself, and, this being so, find ways in which you can profit from that rightness. You will be able to do so if you avoid imposing your own rigid mental structure on the market's behaviour. Once you release yourself from the fear of being wrong, you can observe the market's behaviour from an objective perspective.

Learning to monitor your emotions and your behaviour is the essence of objectivity. Without constantly checking on yourself, you will find you are slipping back into failure habits, no longer accepting that anything that happens is all right because you are confident of your ability to respond appropriately under all circumstances. Make sure you are continuing to focus on the structure of the market as an object of intense interest rather than on the anticipated profit of your trade. If your object of concentration is the money involved, you will be distorting, overlooking, or avoiding the information necessary for you to manage the trade successfully.

5. Watch your risk

To be consistently successful as a trader, a fifth step is to never take a trade that would cause dislocation in your lifestyle or jeopardise your ability to continue trading.

In the *New Market Wizards*, one of the traders interviewed by Schwager, Mark Ritchie, put it this way: 'When you put on a trade, it should be so small that it seems almost a waste of your time.' This is especially true when you're learning about the markets.

Handling anxiety and fear

Douglas makes many useful comments in his book. One that seems particularly perceptive is this: 'The predominate underlying force behind most traders' actions causing prices to move is fear – the fear of missing out and the fear of loss.'

Probably the most damaging downside of fear is the way in which it narrows our perception, severely limiting the range of information to which we can pay attention. If our trade is moving in our direction, we are afraid the market is going to remove our profits, so we zero in on any information that suggests this is happening and we get out too early. Conversely, should our trade be losing, we lock in on information suggesting that it is really doing all right and is likely to recover.

In other words, we allow fear to drastically limit our choices by making us afraid to face all the information that the market is providing. Exiting a trade to limit a loss is not a choice if we systematically block from our awareness any information that would indicate that we are in a losing trade. Staying with a winner to allow profits to run is not a choice if we are overwhelmed with the fear that the market is going to take away our money.

This perception-limited fear is usually a product of one-shot learning. The most usual scenario is that of one disastrous loss, embedded deeply in the memory as a result of the intense negative emotion generated at that time and dramatically interfering with future trading performance. Fortunately, there are a number of ways of coping with this fear, or with any traumatic incident from the past which exerts a continuing negative influence in the present.

Progressive desensitisation

This method can be very effective in reducing the power of a traumatic memory.

Joanne, who had been trading options for a couple of years, is a good illustration of how this method might be employed. She had been selling cash-covered calls for some time with a steady growth in her equity. Naturally, she monitored her positions carefully – except for one occasion when she went on a holiday.

As the positions she held were well out of the money, she felt confident that there would be no drama during her 10-day absence. Unfortunately, Murphy's Law lives on.

The share price of the company in which she had sold the calls surged due to events the market had not anticipated. Joanne's shares were called from her. As she did not own these shares she was faced with going into the market, buying at a considerably higher price than that at which she had sold the calls, and covering her position. The loss was over $25,000, an amount which wiped out her previous profits and put her onto the debit side of the ledger.

Although she was able to cover the position, Joanne lost confidence in her method of investing which had, in the past, been quite profitable. She became more tentative and increasingly anxious about her trading.

To overcome this problem through the use of progressive desensitisation, Joanne created a hierarchy of situations. She began with one that evoked very little anxiety, continued through a range of other situations that evoked increasing levels of anxiety, and concluded with the most fear-evoking incident of all. Her hierarchy looked like this:

▷ Reading books about option trading.

▷ Talking to people about the market.

▷ Reading newspaper articles about the stock market.

▷ Watching a friend making trades.

▷ Studying the option market and making paper trades.

▷ Trading on a very small scale.

▷ Trading on the scale she had done previously.

Joanne imagined the first of these scenes, 'seeing' herself reading a book about option trading. When she was able to do so without feeling anxious, she moved on to the next level of the hierarchy, that of 'seeing' herself talking to friends about the market. Gradually, without putting any pressure on herself, she moved through the hierarchy, step by step, until she was able to imagine herself trading successfully and confidently.

At any stage, should she feel anxious about the situation she was imagining, she would switch her thoughts away to some calming past experience, enjoying its atmosphere of happiness, contentment, and stillness until she felt peaceful and relaxed. She would then return to the scene which had evoked the anxiety and imagine it again until she was able to do so without discomfort. Once this was achieved, Joanne would move onto the next level in the hierarchy. This process was continued until she had contemplated all the hierarchy items in a comfortable way.

Three-part dissociation

Should this progressive desensitisation method have proved unsuccessful, Joanne could have made use of the three-part dissociation technique. Justin, a 43-year-old clerk, had also lost a lot of money over a poor trading decision. He ceased trading at that time but, three years later, wanted to again enter the market. However, he was still haunted by the memory of the loss, which seemed to be constantly lurking at the back of his mind.

Justin sat quietly facing a blank wall, imagining that he could see a movie screen on which was portrayed his younger self just before the disastrous trade occurred. When the picture was clear, Justin visualised himself floating into the movie screen and 'becoming' his younger self, making the whole situation as real as possible. He then relived the original traumatic event, describing it out loud. As he did so, I touched the back of his hand, the idea being to link this touch to the fear-engendering situation. Once Justin finished his description, he floated back into his body.

He then described out loud a time in his life when he felt confident, in control of his environment, joyous, and happy with himself. This very positive feeling was linked to a touch on his elbow. Both these touches, one to the back of the hand and the other to the elbow, are termed 'anchors'. The two anchors were then tested to ensure they revived the two different internal states, one of fear and the other of confident happiness.

To help separate himself from the traumatic picture, on the next viewing, Justin imagined himself sitting behind himself in the chair as he watched, on the screen, his younger self making the losing trade. I triggered the comfort anchor by touching his elbow as he talked about what he saw happening. Once he had finished, I suggested that Justin go to the young man he had been watching on the screen and comfort him. He then returned to the chair.

When Justin was able to do this, I first triggered the negative state with the hand touch, and then the positive state with the elbow touch. I held both these anchors with equal pressure for 20 to 30 seconds, then gradually released the pressure on the negative one until finally I had removed my finger completely. I then transferred control to Justin by having him reach across his body and trigger his elbow anchor himself.

Although I have described this technique as I used it with Justin, it is possible for a person to do it alone, without the help of a psychologist. In this case, the anchors chosen would be ones easy for the person to reach, such as touching the knees or ear lobes. The same thing applies if you want to change using the following approach.

Changing your personal history

Firstly, you need to identify what it is that you wish to change. Then recreate, mentally, the unpleasant feelings associated with the unwanted behaviour pattern. As these feelings strengthen within you, create an anchor, such as a touch to the right knee. By repeating that particular touch, you will be able to recreate that negative situation.

Secondly, explore your experience to discover what resource you now possess that could be 'taken back' into the past to change the unpleasant feelings. This resource might be increased confidence, more trust, greater maturity, or more relaxation; attributes you now have that were not present in the initial, negative situation. One way of identifying such resources is to think of a relatively recent experience you handled very effectively and successfully.

Should you be unable to find a resource which, if applied to the original, unpleasant situation, would have made things better, imagine how an admired person may have handled the situation. This model might be a friend or a character in a book or film, anyone who appears to have the resources you require to improve your situation. As you imagine yourself using the desired resources to achieve your objective, the positive feeling engendered by this success is again anchored, this time, perhaps, with a touch on the left knee. Remember, it is necessary to test that the anchor actually does work, further repetition being required if it does not do so.

The third step involves you touching the first anchor to recreate the unpleasant situation, then touching the second anchor, to bring in the positive feelings of the resource. Hold both anchors for a minute or two and gradually release the pressure on the negative one. Do this very slowly. Rest quietly with eyes closed, taking as long as is necessary for the unpleasant feelings to change under the influence of the positive resource. And change they usually do. Many people feel and 'see' themselves responding differently, successfully, thus creating a new history.

It is then necessary to test the negative anchor to make sure it no longer evokes the undesired feeling state.

You may care to link a colour to your two anchors. Usually, when you enter your negative state you will, if you think about it, be able to identify a colour such as black or brown. For the positive state, the colour is more likely to be yellow or blue. Once you have identified the two colours, when you hold both your anchors you will probably find the two colours blending and, as the process continues, the black or brown fading away to be replaced by the yellow or blue.

The process may be then generalised to any situation, similar to the one changed by the above method, which you are likely to meet in the future. What you are saying to yourself is: "In the future, anytime I experience anything similar to my previous unpleasant situation, I will feel this [touching the resource anchor]."

Kaye's story

To see the technique in action, let's look at Kaye, a 39-year-old woman who was returning to trading after an absence of seven years. Although she attempted to carry out her market analysis in the same relatively successful way as she had done previously, her performance remained at a level considerably inferior to that which she had previously maintained. Naturally enough, this resulted in a diminution of Kaye's self-confidence. Whereas, previously, she was able to give her undivided attention to the task at hand, that of careful consideration of the market, she now found such concentration more difficult as thoughts of failure and losses intruded.

Relaxing herself by concentrating upon her breath and visualising a calming scene, Kaye recalled her difficulty in concentration and the negative feelings this generated. These she anchored through a touch to her right knee. As she did so, a purplish colour was strong in her mind. She then switched her thoughts away to think of something neutral, such as what she was going to prepare for her evening meal. Once she had cleared her mind in this way, she triggered her anchor that recreated the negative emotional state.

Once again she cleared her mind. She then thought of her moment of greatest triumph, the trade which enabled her to pay off the mortgage on her home. In particular, she concentrated on the surge of confidence she felt, a confidence which had led to further improvement in her trading performance. This very positive feeling was anchored by a touch to her left knee, paired with the colour green which spontaneously appeared in her mind. Again the process of mind clearing and testing of the anchor was successfully accomplished.

These two anchors were then touched simultaneously, as explained earlier. After she held both for a few minutes, Kaye gradually withdrew her hand from her right knee. However, when this anchor was tested after about five minutes, some negative feeling and the purplish colour were still present to some extent. Accordingly, a second triggering of both anchors was necessary. Further testing indicated that the negative feelings had disappeared. Kaye's subsequent performance indicated that this technique had helped her regain both her confidence and her concentration, for her trading returned to its previous profitable state.

Focus on the present moment

To some extent, anxiety results from the gap between the present and the future, in that our fears are a function of the way we think about things that are not with us here in the present. Frequently they may be well off in the future. So focus on the present, the thing you have to do now rather than on this fear-provoking image of the future. Instead of concentrating on the large goal of making a fortune out of trading, narrow your focus to the next trade you will make. Once that has been concluded, make the next trade your sub-goal. Breaking down the large task into smaller pieces makes it more manageable and less anxiety-rousing.

Perhaps you will have to work out ways of coping with anxiety if it is interfering with the attainment of these sub-goals. The black box could be helpful here. In your mind, write down whatever is upsetting you on a slip of paper and lock it away in a black box to be dealt with later at a set time, say 3.30 pm that afternoon. When this time arrives, open the black box and deal with the anxiety. It is quite likely that it will no longer seem to be of much importance to you. Separate yourself from these concerns. Don't inflict them upon yourself but set them apart from you.

Acting 'as if'

When you engage the power to change your mood state instead of simply reacting to conditions outside of yourself, your trading and your life take on a new positive force. One of the most effective ways to achieve such a change is to act 'as if' you were feeling differently from the way you are. If you feel sluggish, lethargic, dreary, force yourself to act differently. Put your shoulders back, look up, walk energetically, hum or sing to yourself, and think of something pleasant.

If you are unable to engage this power to be different, find a model. Caroline, a middle-aged housewife, had the intelligence and the knowledge to be a much better trader than she was. What she lacked was belief in herself. As a result, she was influenced in her trading decisions by other people and newspaper stories providing opinions less accurate than those she came to from her own studies of the market. For some time, Caroline attempted to act as if she was more assertive in acting on her own beliefs. However, she wasn't able to keep up this act with sufficient consistency to change her behaviour to any marked extent.

One of the people who often influenced Caroline's decisions was very assertive, with a genuine belief in herself. So Caroline used her as a model, acting as if she were the other person whenever she needed to act on her decisions. However, she was very selective, modelling only the self-belief, nothing else, for that was the only characteristic she felt she was lacking. It is both undesirable and unnecessary to become someone else. All that is required is to find someone who possesses the particular characteristic you feel that you lack, and to then use that person as a model as to how you can acquire that characteristic.

INSTANT ANXIETY MANAGEMENT

Sometimes we need to drain off anxiety instantly. One way of doing so is to imagine a blackboard 'out there' somewhere close to you, on which you write, mentally, as briefly as possible, whatever is worrying you. Then wipe the blackboard clean. Should the anxiety-provoking thoughts reoccur, put them out on the blackboard again and wipe them away. Do not allow such thoughts to remain in your head. Separate yourself from them by placing them 'out there'. They are no longer part of you.

Alternatively, you could use a 'mantra', words or sounds continually repeated to provide a focus of concentration which overrides the anxiety-provoking thoughts. Single words or sounds such as 'calm' and 'om' are popular, or a sentence such as 'I am calm, relaxed, and confident' could be used. If unwanted thoughts intrude, gently bring your mind back to its focus on the mantra as it revolves around in your mind.

Channelling your anxiety and tension into an imaginary oblong rod is another alternative. This becomes a concrete symbol, something you can manipulate. As long as you allow your anxiety to be abstract, free-floating, it is very difficult to alleviate it. However, once you give it a shape and size, as you do with the symbol of the oblong rod, you can compress it, making it smaller and smaller until it becomes completely insignificant. At this point you can throw it away.

It is comforting to have well-practised procedures available for immediate effect when you need them. The ones described so far – the oblong rod, a screen, or a secret place – have some specific content but it is also possible to focus entirely upon the actual process, without any regard to content at all, as a means of handling anxiety.

Symptom prescription

This technique, labelled symptom substitution or paradoxical intention, seems contrary to common sense for it involves directing people to do the very thing they have already been doing. However, its great value is that, because it appears to fly in the face of common sense, it will often succeed when more logical, commonsense approaches fail. Because individuals are asked to do a virtual about-face and actually intensify their symptoms, they are given an entirely different perspective on their problems. The reasonable, rational treatment has not been successful, so perhaps an apparently unreasonable, irrational approach may work, particularly with a symptom that seems rather irrational anyway. At its best, the technique involves a change in attitude from one of fear of the symptom to one of laughter about it, and there is no lack of evidence supporting the effectiveness of symptom prescription in resolving a wide range of human problems.

The use of symptom prescription in the trading area can be seen with Andrew, an experienced part-time trader who had become highly erratic in his behaviour. In particular, he no longer set aside specific times to study the market, had no set routine for such study when he did get around to it, and no real organisation in his life generally.

During the day, he spent much of his time concentrating on trying to be as disorganised as possible. In particular, he focused on being totally erratic in his trading study, in that he deliberately chose a different study time each evening, and went about it differently each time. The harder he tried to do so, the more his regularity improved and a definite routine emerged, a circumstance which illustrates the most important property of symptom substitution – control is given to the person using it. The involuntary becomes voluntary, so that unwanted behaviour may be, at best, entirely eliminated or, at least, considerably reduced. Although Andrew was not able to completely overcome occasional waywardness, he certainly became more organised in his life generally.

The three-finger technique

Another way to facilitate improved use of the mental facilities is one of the approaches used by the practitioners of Silva Mind Control. They follow the approach suggested in this book, that it is desirable to establish anchors while in the relaxed or alpha state. The way of entering this state that they recommend is to close your eyes, look upward at an angle of about 20 degrees beneath the closed lids, and use the 3 to 1, 10 to 1 method. This involves imagining that, about six feet out in front of you, is a mental screen. On this screen, as you exhale, you visualise the number three. This is repeated three times, after which the number two is coupled with three exhalations of breath. The same procedure is followed for the number one. Then the number ten is visualised on the screen, again linked with the letting go of the breath. This number is 'seen' only once, followed by nine, eight, and the other numbers down to one, when the process is deemed to be complete.

The actual relaxation method used to attain the alpha state is immaterial, but the method outlined above is usually quite effective. However, if this does not appeal to you, numerous alternatives may be found in other chapters of this book. Once in this state you repeat, 'Whenever I join my fingers together like this [at this point the tips of the first and second finger of either hand are placed against the thumb] I will instantly reach the level of mind to accomplish whatever I desire'. This procedure is repeated several times each day for the period of a week. At the end of this time, Silva believes the conditioning process to be complete and the signal ready for use.

A trader of stock market options, Russell, used this technique to restore his ability to concentrate which had abated somewhat as he grew older. Now, at 53, he was finding it increasingly difficult to keep his mind focused upon finding the over- and under-valued options which had been the basis of his prosperity. He linked the three-fingers signal to his desire to concentrate intensely. After a week of conditioning through the Silva approach, Russell was able to summon his previous level of concentration at will. At any time during his study of option possibilities, should he feel his attention was wandering, he would place his fingers together to summon the focus he needed in order to be successful.

Diagnostic Trance

Yet another systematic way of encouraging people in the use of their inner resources to solve problems is the Diagnostic Trance. People sit quietly, eyes closed, physically relaxed, concentrating upon the unpleasant sensations or feelings associated with their problem. By turning inward in order to focus upon these internal events, they tend to drift into a trance state.

While mentally observing these unpleasant sensations, they describe, in a somewhat detached manner, the thoughts and images that are present in their minds. They make no effort to control these in any way, simply allowing associated memories to surface quite spontaneously. Usually they reveal a pattern of thinking, a series of images, or even a specific memory which is creating the problem. Sometimes these are in the form of visual images of previously forgotten incidents, usually of a traumatic nature. On other occasions they may take the form of a voice repeating a particular negative statement.

Once people have been able to identify the source or sources of their unpleasant feelings, they attempt to find a thought or image that is sufficiently powerful to remove or displace the negative material. On many occasions, people find that they have the inner resources needed to solve their problem but, until given the opportunity provided by the Diagnostic Trance, they were unaware that they possessed these resources. However, the Diagnostic Trance procedure appears to encourage the spontaneous emergence of creative solutions, as the following case study illustrates.

George's story

George, a 38-year-old currency trader, was, in most respects, a relatively relaxed person. However, this relaxation did not extend to holding a position over weekends. Past experience had shown him that holding such positions usually resulted in greater profits than if he closed out his trades before the weekend, yet in this situation, he became extremely anxious, an anxiety which was reflected in an accelerated pulse rate, profuse perspiration, and stomach disturbance. His sleep pattern would be disturbed by unpleasant dreams, early waking, and difficulty in falling asleep again.

To identify the specific nature of George's problem, the Diagnostic Trance procedure was employed. He was encouraged to sit quietly, eyes closed, relaxed and comfortable, watching the flow of his breath and allowing himself to let go. As he did so, his mind drifted back to occasions when he felt it was necessary to hold a large position over a weekend, and he became increasingly aware of the unpleasant sensations associated with this situation. Because of the vividness with which most people recall past experiences while in a trance state, he mentally re-experienced his anxiety, accelerated heart beat, and feelings of general discomfort.

George described these unpleasant sensations that accompanied the imaginative recreations of holding positions over the weekend, then sought a thought or image which would have the power to negate such feelings. He did so in a very relaxed way, not pressuring himself, but simply allowing his thoughts to drift lazily. Many images flowed through his mind until one with considerable power emerged quite spontaneously. This was an occasion that took place when he was in his late teens. While walking his dog, he witnessed a car accident in which the driver was knocked unconscious. The car was on fire and, acting instinctively, without thought for his own safety, George raced to the car and was able to pull the driver clear before the flames reached him. As he recalled this event, George felt a surge of very positive feeling.

The power of this success imagery was sufficient to neutralise the effect of the previous unpleasant feelings. As he rested in the trance state, George switched back and forth between the two sets of thoughts and images, developing confidence in his ability to use the positive feelings – engendered by the bravery experience – to obliterate the negative feelings of holding weekend positions. While he was doing so, it was suggested to him that, in future, whenever the thought of holding a position over the weekend crossed his mind, he would immediately bring to mind the image of himself saving the driver and his own sense of pride in his achievement.

CHAPTER 13

WRAPPING IT UP

'An unexamined life is not worth living.'

– Socrates

All the techniques outlined in this book have worked for many people on many occasions. That is not to say that every one of them will work for you. It is up to you to try them out to find which ones produce for you the changes you desire. As you do find these, they will enable you to overcome the common psychological errors made by traders and achieve the solutions diagrammed below.

Psychological errors

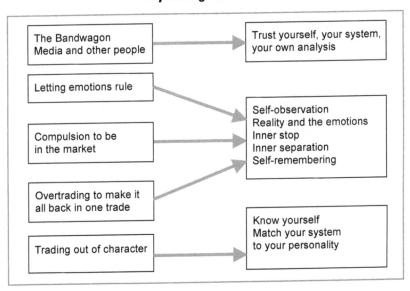

This diagram summarises the message of this book, that psychological factors are as important, if not more so, than possession of a proven trading system and knowledge of money-management rules. The psychological errors that appear in the diagram all stem from the lack of emotional discipline. Helping you to achieve such discipline has been the purpose of this book. I have no doubt that once you achieve such emotional control, the trade wins will surely flow.

LOUISE'S THOUGHTS

I'm sure you can now see why I treasure Harry's words, and his presence in my life. Over the last couple of decades, many times I've found myself turning to Harry's wisdom to help me through situations I'm facing in my trading. His book can be your guide, during times of triumph and during times of confusion in the markets. Due to Harry's efforts in helping people improve their trading mindset, many traders have managed to leap-frog their trading hurdles and come out on top.

I can tell you with 100 per cent certainty that in my first three years of trading, while I was trying to crack the code, I never realised where I would end up just a few short years down the track. I shudder to think where I would be if I had given up and quit this exciting trading game.

Realise the **gold** we've handed you in this book. Remember the importance of persistence. Refuse to give up – smash your rear-view mirrors and forgive yourself for your past mistakes. The wealthiest, happiest, and most effective traders on the planet work as hard on themselves as they do on their trading systems.

If you're still waiting for the profits to come pouring in, it may all be closer than you think. My advice? Devote yourself to your education. Don't neglect the opportunities at hand – in either your trading, or your life.

Now that you've read it through once, I suggest you keep it with you and regularly turn back to sections that resonated with you.

Chris Tate, Harry Stanton, and I wish you all the best.

Also by Dr Harry Stanton

Psychology Secrets and *Relaxation for Traders* CD sets – available from **www.tradinggame.com.au**.

Psychology Secrets
by Chris Tate, Louise Bedford, and Dr Harry Stanton

This double CD set will take you through the 10 most common trading mistakes and explore practical solutions that you can apply to boost your profits. You can't afford to miss out on implementing these strategies. By listening to this CD set, you will learn how to overcome trading for the thrill factor, reliance on subjective sources, overtrading, self-sabotage, and much, much more.

Relaxation for Traders
by Louise Bedford and Dr Harry Stanton

Stress, racing heart, sweaty palms? They're all a part of being a share trader, right?

Actually, the best traders have discovered techniques that allow them to trade calmly, with confidence and clarity. If you would like to learn how to trade with focused concentration, assurance, and precision, it is probably simpler than you ever believed possible! This audio CD will take you through relaxation methods designed to calm your thoughts. These relaxation techniques can assist with a variety of trading challenges, including not acting on stop losses, difficulty in adhering to a trading plan, and results-related anxiety. It is separated into four tracks:

- ▸ Track 1: Introduction
- ▸ Track 2: Mental Control with Harry Stanton
- ▸ Track 3: Effective Trading with Louise Bedford
- ▸ Track 4: Unleash the Unconscious with Harry Stanton

Order your CD sets today from www.tradinggame.com.au

Somewhere inside you there is a brilliant trader wanting to come out.

From the trading desk of Louise Bedford …

Louise Bedford here.

I'm on a quest!

A quest to create as many happy, independent, wealthy and skilled share traders as possible.

Make no mistake – successfully trading the sharemarket is one of the most valuable skills you'll ever learn. Once you know how to trade, **no-one can ever take this ability away from you.**

Louise Bedford
Your Trading Mentor

It's with you for life. The rewards will keep rolling in for you and your entire family.

Register now on my website and I'll give you my free 5-part e-course and help you **finally nail the simple trading secrets necessary to make your profits soar.**

INDEX

BIBLIOGRAPHY

Bandler, R. *Using Your Brain*. Moab, Utah: Real People Press, 1985.

Bandler, R. *Time For a Change*. Cupertino, Calif.: Meta Publications, 1993.

Bernstein, J. *Beyond the Investor's Quotient*. New York: Wiley, 1986.

Douglas, M. *The Disciplined Trader*. New York: New York Institute of Finance, 1990.

Gallwey, T. *The Inner Game of Tennis*. New York: Random House, 1974.

Gallwey, T. *Inner Tennis*. New York: Random House, 1976.

Elder, A. *Trading for a Living*. New York: Wiley & Sons, 1993.

Robbins, A. *Awaken the Giant Within*. New York: Fireside, 1991.

Schwager, J. D. *The New Market Wizards*. New York: Harper Business, 1992.

Lightning Source UK Ltd.
Milton Keynes UK
UKHW02f2340090218

317633UK00004B/487/P